Library of
Davidson College

VOID

The American Revolutionary Series

BRITISH ACCOUNTS
OF THE
AMERICAN REVOLUTION

*The American Revolutionary Series
is published in cooperation with
The Boston Public Library*

Letters of Hugh Earl Percy From Boston and New York, 1774-1776

Edited by
CHARLES KNOWLES BOLTON

With a New Introduction and Preface by
GEORGE ATHAN BILLIAS

GREGG PRESS
Boston 1972

This is a complete photographic reprint of a work
first published in Boston by Charles E. Goodspeed in 1902.
Reproduced from an original copy in the Boston Public Library.

First Gregg Press edition published 1972.

Printed in permanent/durable acid-free paper in
The United States of America.

923.542
N878zl

Library of Congress Cataloging in Publication Data

Northumberland, Hugh Percy, 2d Duke of, 1742-1817.
    Letters of Hugh, Earl Percy, from Boston and New
York, 1774-1776.

    (American Revolutionary series. British accounts of
the American Revolution)
    Reprint of the 1902 ed.
    1. United States—History—Revolution—Personal
narratives—Brittish. 2. United States—History—revolution—British forces. I. Bolton, Charles Knowles,
1867-1950, ed. II. Series: American Revolutionary
series. III. Series: British accounts of the American
Revolution.
E275.N87   1972   973.3'41'0924 [B]   72-8731
ISBN 0-8398-0190-4

BRITISH ACCOUNTS OF THE AMERICAN REVOLUTION

THE STORY OF the American Revolution remains a rather one-sided one, even after almost two hundred years. There are many reasons why this is so, not the least of them being the general unavailability of certain important British historical source books. This series, *British Accounts of the American Revolution,* aims to make more accessible some primary and secondary source materials that heretofore were out-of-print, available only in abridged editions, or found mainly in rare book collections.

Institutions tend to reflect the societies from which they spring, and the British navy, army, and war cabinet were no exceptions to the rule. British society, being hierarchically-minded and class conscious, tended to produce military organizations that were microcosms of the society at large. It should be no surprise, therefore, to find that most of these accounts represent the view from the top, so to speak—the writings, memoirs, and biographies of British admirals, generals, and ministers who directed the war effort.

The navy was Britain's main line of defense and offense throughout the eighteenth century, and many of the books in this series are devoted to naval history. Two of the multi-volume sets—Robert Beatson's *Naval and Military Memoirs of Great Britain, from 1727-1783* and James Ralfe's *The Naval Biography of Great Britain*—are regarded as classics by some historians. The two biographies of Admiral George

B. Rodney by Godfrey B. Mundy and David Hannay, on the other hand, are treated with great caution by scholars. Thomas White's *Naval Researches,* although seemingly highly specialized, takes up one of the most celebrated controversies regarding naval tactics of the Revolutionary War.

The British army comes in for its fair share of attention. Edward B. DeFonblanque's biography of John Burgoyne remains an important explanation for the general's conduct in the Saratoga campaign in 1777. The journals and orderly books of Lieutenant James M. Hadden of the Royal Artillery, however, give us glimpses of that same campaign from another point of view. Sir Hugh Percy's letters from Boston and New York from 1774 to 1776 record some impressions of American reactions early in the war, while Colonel Stephen Kemble's journals of army orders enable us to fix the exact location of most British units in the New York City area from 1775 to 1778.

The most significant books in this series for the research scholar are the volumes issued initially by the Historical Manuscripts Commission of Great Britain. These works present the writings of some of Britain's most important government and military leaders at the time of the Revolutionary War. Two volumes—*Report on the Manuscripts of Mrs. Stopford-Sackville of Drayton House Northamptonshire*—are concerned mainly with the papers of Lord George Germain, the cabinet minister primarily responsible for British strategy in the American theater of operations. Another volume reprints many papers of the Earl of Dartmouth, Secretary of State for the Colonies from August, 1772, to November, 1775. A four-volume set—*Report of the American Manuscripts in the Royal Institution of Great Britain*—contains the headquarters papers of the successive commanders-in-chief of the British army during the war.

The publication of this series should help to redress the existing imbalance of historical sources in America on the subject, and to make it possible to present the British side of the struggle in more meaningful terms.

PREFACE

HUGH PERCY (1742-1817), the British general, was known by the courtesy title of Earl Percy during his years of service in America. He was the eldest son of Hugh Smithson Percy, who became the first Duke of Northumberland. Upon the death of his mother in 1776, he succeeded to the barony of Percy.

Lord Percy had seen extended military service prior to coming to America. His military career began when he was gazetted as an ensign in the Twenty-fourth Foot, but became a captain in the Eighty-fifth Regiment the same year. Fighting on the continent in the Seven Years' War, he served under Prince Ferdinand of Brunswick and distinguished himself in the battles of Bergen and Minden as a lieutenant colonel commanding the One Hundred and Eleventh Regiment. In 1762 he entered the Grenadier Guards, and two years later was promoted to colonel and appointed aide-de-camp to George III.

Lord Percy's political views were derived in large part from his parents. His father had voted against the Stamp Act, and showed in other ways that he disapproved of Britain's colonial policy. After being elected to Parliament himself in 1763, Lord Percy was admitted to the King's private circle largely on the basis of his marriage to Lord Bute's daughter. But he kept his connections to the court loose because he disagreed with the King's policies with respect to America.

Although presumably opposed to the idea of military coercion, Lord Percy embarked for America in the spring of 1774 to accept a military post in Boston. His letters back to his family, friends, and colleagues reprinted here are important for the insights they provide into the political and military situation at the time. He thought highly, for example of General Thomas Gage, declaring that he "has done his duty with great coolness and firmness." His views of the colonists were shrewd and penetrating: "The people in this part of the country are in general made up of rashness & timidity. Quick & violent in their determinations, they are fearful in the execution of them (unless, indeed they are quite certain of meeting little or no opposition, & then, like all other cowards, they are cruel and tyrannical). To hear them talk, you would imagine that they would attack us & demolish us every night; & yet, whenever we appear, they are frightened out of their wits."

On the day of Lexington and Concord, he led the relief column that saved the retreating British force from probable annihilation. Once again, his estimate of the American fighting qualities were to the point. "Whoever looks upon them as an irregular mob, will find himself much mistaken. They have men amongst them who know very well what they are about, having been employed as Rangers agst the Indians & Canadians, & this country being cov[ere]d w[ith] wood, and hilly, is very advantageous for their method of fighting."

Lord Percy later commanded a division at the battle of Long Island on August 27, 1776, and wrote a long letter to his father about the British victory. Although his letters in this volume end on November 3, 1776, Lord Percy was to remain in America until mid-1777. He participated in the attack on Fort Washington in November, 1776, the capture of Rhode Island in December of that same year, and assumed command of that post when General Henry Clinto went on leave to England. After numerous disagreements with General William Howe, the commander-in-chief, Lord Percy returned to England in June, 1777.

His letters constitute an important collection primarily for the information they provide into the period immediately preceding the outbreak of hostilities.

George Athan Billias
Clark University

LETTERS OF
HUGH *EARL* PERCY

HUGH *EARL* **PERCY.**
AFTER THE MEZZOTINT BY VALENTINE GREEN.
S.L.SMITH. SC.

Letters

OF

HUGH *EARL* PERCY

from

BOSTON and NEW YORK

1774–1776

Edited by

CHARLES KNOWLES BOLTON

BOSTON
CHARLES E. GOODSPEED
1902

Copyright, 1902, *by Charles E. Goodspeed*

D. B. UPDIKE, THE MERRYMOUNT PRESS, BOSTON

In Memory of
THE REV^D EDWARD GRIFFIN PORTER

PREFACE

THE letters which are printed in this volume have been gathered from several sources. Those from the reports of the Royal Commission on Historical Manuscripts are indicated by footnotes. Letters numbered i, ii, x, xii, xvi, xxiii, xxvii, xxviii, and xxix are from the manuscripts owned by the Boston Public Library and are reprinted by permission of the Trustees from the Bulletin for January, 1892. The letters not referred to above were copied by the Rev. Edward Griffin Porter during a visit of a few days in 1878 to the late Duke of Northumberland at Alnwick Castle. To Miss Gertrude Montague Graves I am indebted for bringing these letters to my notice, and for the following account of Mr. Porter's stay at Alnwick, as described by him before the Abigail Adams Chapter (Boston) of the Daughters of the American Revolution:

"While preparing a history of Lexington, Massachusetts, for the Centennial Celebration of the battle of Lexington, the late Edward G. Porter, pas-

PREFACE

tor of the Hancock Church in that town, entered into correspondence with the Duke of Northumberland. Through this correspondence, a mutual regard grew up between Mr. Porter and the Duke, which resulted in a visit by the former to Alnwick Castle.

"While a guest there, a certain alcove and shelf were pointed out to him; after glancing over numerous books, he espied, in an obscure corner, what proved to be a tin box covered thickly with dust, and tied with a frayed blue ribbon. In answer to inquiry, the Duke's Librarian told him that the box contained letters, but he never remembered to have seen it opened. It was dusted and opened forthwith, disclosing a budget of faded and yellow letters, the veritable ones that Earl Percy had written to his father, beginning at the moment of his landing in Boston, and ending at the time of his return to England. Mr. Porter had the satisfaction, with the permission of his host, of spending that day and the two succeeding ones in copying these letters."

Mr. Porter wrote a letter to the Lexington Minute-Man, dated at Alnwick September 27,

PREFACE

1878, and printed October 14th, in which he said: "Percy's letters, and many other family documents, have been generously placed at my disposal by His Grace the Duke of Northumberland. I have made numerous extracts, touching upon events of 1775, which I may give to friends at home, in some form, after my return." His sudden death in February, 1900, occurred before they had been given to the public in any printed form, and before he had expressed any wish concerning their publication. His sister, Miss Ellen Carruth, very kindly allowed me to make this use of her brother's copies after I had submitted them to the present Duke, at whose request certain references to family matters have been omitted. To Mr. Lindsay Swift and to other friends I am indebted for helpful suggestions.

Pound Hill, Shirley, April, 1902.

CONTENTS

Introduction	15
Letters of Earl Percy.	
I. To the Rev. Thomas Percy, April 17, 1774	25
Before sailing for America.	
II. To the Rev. Thomas Percy, May 8, 1774	26
From on board the 'Symetry.'	
III. To the Duke of Northumberland, July 5, 1774	26
Arrival in Boston.	
IV. To the Duke of Northumberland, July 27, 1774	27
The inhabitants; the climate.	
V. To Henry Reveley, Esq., August 8, 1774	30
The climate and the people.	
VI. To the Duke of Northumberland, August 15, 1774	31
Trees; products of the soil; local events.	
VII. To General Harvey (?), August 21, 1774	35
Effect of the Regulation Acts.	
VIII. To the Duke of Northumberland, September 12, 1774	37
"Things are now drawing to a crisis."	
IX. To . . . . . . , October 10, 1774	39
Trouble in Lord Percy's regiment.	
X. To the Rev. Thomas Percy, October 27, 1774	40
XI. To General Harvey (?), November 1, 1774	41
Military preparations on both sides.	
XII. To the Rev. Thomas Percy, November 25, 1774	43
State of affairs; request for books.	

CONTENTS

XIII. To Henry Reveley, Esq., December 6, 1774   45
"Reinforcement gives great spirits."

XIV. To Grey Cooper, Esq., after December 13, 1774   46
Seizure of powder at Newcastle.

XV. To General Harvey, February 9, 1775   47

XVI. To the Rev. Thomas Percy, April 8, 1775   48
Conditions in Boston.

XVII. To Governor Gage, April 20, 1775   49
Official account of the retreat from Lexington.

XVIII. To General Harvey, April 20, 1775   52
Part of an unofficial account of the retreat, with other papers.

XIX. To the Duke of Northumberland, April 20, 1775   54
The retreat from Lexington.

XX. To Henry Reveley, Esq., May, 1775   55
The enemy burn houses and a schooner.

XXI. To the Duke of Northumberland, June 19, 1775   56
Battle of Bunker Hill.

XXII. To General Harvey (?), July 28, 1775   58
Comments on the campaign.

XXIII. To the Rev. Thomas Percy, August 12, 1775   59

XXIV. To the Duke of Northumberland, August 18, 1775   61
"Their aim is independence."

XXV. To Henry Reveley, Esq., October 29, 1775   61
Preparations for winter.

XXVI. To General Haldimand, December 14, 1775   62
"The rebels have been too fortunate."

CONTENTS

XXVII. To the Rev. Thomas Percy, January 7, 1776   64
Affairs at Headquarters.

XXVIII. To the Rev. Thomas Percy, June 1, 1776   66
"Flight of the rebels from before Quebeck."

XXIX. To the Duke of Northumberland, September 1, 1776   67
Battle of Long Island.

XXX. To Lord George Germain, September 2, 1776   70
Battle of Long Island.

XXXI. To a Gentleman in London, September 4, 1776   71
Battle of Long Island.

XXXII. To Lord George Germain, October 30, 1776   72
Manœuvres at New York.

XXXIII. To Henry Reveley, Esq., November 3, 1776   75
Manœuvres at New York.

Note in Conclusion   79

Index   85

INTRODUCTION

HUGH PERCY, known during the years of his service in America as Earl Percy, was born August 14, 1742, in the parish of Saint George's, Hanover Square, London, the son of Sir Hugh and Lady Elizabeth Smithson. His parents were later the first Duke and Duchess of Northumberland of this line. The heiress of the ancient House of Percy had married in 1685 Charles Seymour, sixth duke of Somerset. Their son Algernon Seymour, the seventh duke of Somerset, and by special creation in honor of his maternal descent, Earl of Northumberland, had a daughter Lady Elizabeth Seymour, who on the death of her brother, without issue, became heiress of the Percy barony and of great family estates.

Lady Betty gave her heart to a young Yorkshire baronet, Sir Hugh Smithson, before her parents had consented to their engagement. "I must honestly confess to you," she wrote to her mother, "that had it met with my Pappa's approbation and yours, I should very willingly have consented to it. Nay, I shall not scruple to own that I have a partiality for him." Her health began to fail under the delays that followed. At last consent came, and 'Sir Hugh and Betty' were married in July, 1740. Sir Hugh brought to the alliance an ambition, fed by his wife's pride in her Percy blood, to revive the decaying greatness of the Percies in the north. In 1750, upon

INTRODUCTION

succeeding his father-in-law as Earl of Northumberland, he took the name of Percy. In 1766 he was created Earl Percy (the title used by his eldest son) and Duke of Northumberland. The Duke and Duchess rebuilt castles, fostered agriculture, bettered the condition of the farmers, and for twenty years planted over a thousand trees annually.

This was the work accomplished by the parents of Lord Percy, and much that was attractive in his character, saving his name from the abuse heaped upon other British officers in America, is to be traced to his father and his mother. The Duke had voted against the Stamp Act, and in other ways he continued to show disapproval of his party's colonial policy. The son was in sympathy with his father's views.

Although opposed to the American war, Lord Percy embarked for Boston in the spring of 1774, and was for a time in command of the forces there. His conduct in America was closely watched by his political opponents. A letter written at this time was printed in the London Chronicle in October, 1774, when he was put forward as a candidate for re-election to Parliament from Westminster. A few words may not be out of place in regard to the spirited contest which excited the City for days. The Chronicle for September 29–October 1 contained an announcement to the Freeholders of the City and Liberty of Westminster that two gentlemen of fortune and honor were resolved to offer themselves as candidates, and earnestly requested the citizens to make no promises of votes

INTRODUCTION

and influence. On Tuesday, the 4th of October, a meeting of inhabitants and electors was held in Westminster Hall, a chairman was selected, candidates were proposed, and by a show of hands, Lords Mountmorres and Mahon were declared elected. The former in an "elegant speech" thanked his friends, saying that he felt himself to be in a situation "similar to that of Pompey soliciting the suffrages of the Roman Citizens; so, like that generous Roman, he would, if necessary, expire in defence of the liberties of his constituents and country." Lord Mahon declared that he feared "no Court, no minister." They were then proposed as joint candidates against any others, and joined hands.

At the same time the "worthy electors" were requested, in a card dated October 7th, to favor Lord Percy and Lord Thomas Pelham Clinton, and the canvass began. A notice in the Chronicle for October 11th, signed "*The* MAJORITY *of the* CITY *of* WESTMINSTER'S SOBER INHABITANTS," called upon the candidates (those needy Strangers in particular, with whose worthless characters and persons most of the sober inhabitants are unacquainted) to desist from hiring mobs or bribing worthless people to behave rudely, and promising their votes to the two most peaceably disposed candidates.

The contest now became bitter, and Lord Percy was accused of joining the ministerial band of cut-throats in America.[1] His friends then published the following address,

[1] B. Franklin to Galloway, *October* 12, 1774; *Works, edited by Bigelow, vol. v., page* 371.

INTRODUCTION

and, as will be seen, they incorporated part of a letter from Lord Percy, dated August 10th:

"*To the Worthy Independent Electors of*
WESTMINSTER

MANY scandalous reflections have been thrown out against LORD PERCY for doing his duty as an officer, in accompanying his regiment to North America. But surely this spirited conduct deserves applause rather than censure; for it would have ill become the distinguished name he bears, to have declined any service where his honour was concerned. It is well known his Lordship disapproved those very measures which rendered the present service necessary: besides, he had no reason to suppose he was to have gone to Boston, his first destination being to Florida. And the humanity of his disposition cannot be doubted, after the remarkable proof he gave of it when his regiment lately went abroad, in hiring transports at his own charge to carry over the Soldiers' wives, fitting out them and their children with every thing necessary for the voyage, at the expence of 700£. With regard to his treatment of the Americans themselves, the prudence and moderation of his Lordship's conduct appears in a letter lately received by a Gentleman in this town, who is ready to shew the original, which is dated August 10th, and contains the following remarkable passage.

'I am well with the people of Boston, even with the Select Men. When the people come with complaints, I hear them with patience; and if they are just ones, I take care they shall be immediately redressed, assuring them that we are come to protect the peaceable inhabitants, not to injure them; and that as we are determined to enforce obedience to the laws in other people, we shall be ever ready and desirous to be the first to obey them ourselves.'

As to his Lordship's parliamentary conduct, it has been always constitutional, free, and independent."[1]

Notices now appeared frequently, calling upon the elec-

---
[1] *The London Chronicle for* 1774: *October* 11–13, *page* 356.

INTRODUCTION

tors to support Percy and Clinton, and naming the polling places in each parish. The result of the poll was chronicled from day to day. On October 12th the vote stood: Percy, 658; Clinton, 612; Mountmorres, 270; Mahon, 222; Cotes, 84. Lords Mahon and Mountmorres spoke on the hustings to encourage their followers, and professed a belief that the advantage of the opposition was "like a fire of straw" that would soon burn out. Voters were obliged to swear that they had not cast a ballot before and had not been bribed. They were exhorted to keep the peace and avoid intimidation. Rioting and disorder continued, and Clinton called upon his friends to prevent violence, the vote for Clinton and Percy meanwhile steadily gaining upon that of their opponents. Clinton in later notices expressed regrets that he and his colleague had not been able to call personally on every voter, urged his friends to vote jointly for Percy and himself, and not to delay action. On the 18th the City was said to be laboring under great agitation, as a result of the length of the poll.[1] By the 20th Clinton's notices filled a column of the paper, and he urged the electors to exert their "kind and generous zeal" to make their "extraordinary success" so much the more brilliant. Two days later

---

[1] *Horace Walpole wrote to Sir Horace Mann, October 22, 1774: Wilkes "has met with a heroine to stem the tide of his conquests; who, though not of Arc, nor a pucelle, is a true Joan in spirit, style, and manners. This is her Grace of Northumberland, who has carried the mob of Westminster from him; sitting daily in the midst of Covent-Garden; and will elect her son [Earl Percy] and Lord Thomas Clinton, against Wilkes's two candidates, Lord Mahon and Lord Mountmorres." (Letters, edited by Cunningham, 1866, vol. vi., page 136.)*

INTRODUCTION

Lord Mahon declared from the hustings in Covent Garden that they were willing to set a day for closing the poll, but that their opponents (whose vote was double their own) kept the town "in warm-water." His colleague, who had once compared himself with Pompey the Great, was now, it would appear, called "Pompey the less" in an epigram on the three Pompeys. Lord North's interest in the election is shown by a note from him to Lord Carlisle, dated at Bushy Park, October 23, 1774. It reads: "Having heard that Mr. Delmé is returned to Town, I should be much obliged to your Lordship if you would be so good as to desire him to go over to Covent Garden at any time before Wednesday, and vote for Lord Percy and Lord Thomas Clinton. As the polling is now very slack, he will not be detained five minutes at the hustings."[1] The determination of the Government to make the victory as effective as possible is well shown by the willingness of the Prime Minister to take this trouble to gain a single vote when his candidates were already far ahead of their adversaries, and the polls were near to closing.

When the poll finally closed, at noon on the 26th of October, the vote stood:

For Earl Percy	4994
Lord Pelham Clinton	4744
Lord Mountmorres	2531
Lord Mahon	2342
Humphry Cotes	130

[1] *Historical Manuscripts Commission*, 15th report, part vi., page 280 (*MSS. at Castle Howard*).

INTRODUCTION

The family and friends of Lord Percy prepared an address of gratitude to the electors for the handsome support which he had received.

Lord Percy served with distinction at the retreat from Lexington, and in the campaign about New York, leading his men with spirit at the attack upon Fort Washington in November, 1776; but his inability to agree with Howe led him in 1777 to obtain a recall. He had been made a Major-General in America July 11, 1775 (the commission was signed "at our Court at St. James, 22d June"), and received the same rank in the army September 29th; he became a Lieutenant-General in America March 26, 1776 (his commission was dated at the war office March 23d), and Lieutenant-General in the army August 29, 1777.

Earl Percy inherited his father's dukedom in 1786, and received many offices and honors before his death on July 10, 1817. His first alliance with the daughter of Lord Bute ended in unhappiness in 1779.[1] The same year he married Frances Julia Burrell, sister of his younger brother's wife, and by her he left two sons, who succeeded him as third and fourth dukes of Northumberland.

With his men Percy was popular. His mother wrote in 1770: "I admire you for marching with your regiment; I dare say you are the only man of your rank who ever performed such a journey on foot." He expected obedience and

[1] *Walpole to Sir Horace Mann, May 9, 1778; also letter of July 9, 1779.*

INTRODUCTION

faithfulness from his men, and in return showed a deep interest in their welfare, furnishing clothing and food on occasions, and caring for the widows of those who fell. He was simple and retiring by nature, although not forgetful of the ceremonies required by one in his rank and social station. To his close friends and their children he showed a warm heart.

Almost all Englishmen in 1775 failed to understand the temper of the American people. This is true of Lord Percy during the period covered by the early letters; he soon came to take a calmer view, and it is unfortunate that his later letters are not more numerous. Members of the family who came after him have ever shown a friendly good-will toward America.

LETTERS

I

To the Rev. Thomas Percy

Kinsale, Ap^l. 17th. 1774.

Dear D^R.

THANKS to you for your Letter which I received on my Arrival here. Tho' I wrote by the last Post to my Father, & have nothing to say yet I could not help setting down just to inform you that We are still here, nor have we as yet got any Intelligence of the Transports. However as the Wind is fair, We have reason to expect Them every Moment. Our Orders, with regard to our Encamping at Boston, you know in London full as well if not better than we do, as I find we are to have eight Reg^{ts}. there, I fancy severity is intended. Surely the People of Boston are not Mad enough to think of opposing us. Headiness & Temper will I hope set things in that Quarter to rights, & Genl. Gage is the proper Man to do it. Adieu my Dear D^r. & be assured I am

Your sincere Friend
Percy.

To
The Rev^d. D^r. Percy,[1]
Northumberland House
London.

Free
Percy

---

[1] *Rev. Thomas Percy, to whom many of the letters here printed were addressed, was the son of a grocer at Bridgnorth, in Shropshire, and claimed connection with the House of Percy. His Reliques of Ancient English Poetry had already appeared, and his reputation as a scholar brought him friends among persons of influence. Dr. Percy's loyalty to Northumberland and the Percies made*

PERCY LETTERS

II

To the Rev. Thomas Percy

On Board the Symetry, May 8*th*. 1774.

Dear D^r.

WE are at last on board, & shall sail directly. I should think myself much obliged to you if you would send me over the English Votes constantly to Boston. My Newspapers the Porter will forward as usual. I am so cold—I can scarce hold my Pen, & if I could it & the Ink are so bad I can hardly make the Letter legible. Adieu my Dear D^r. & believe me

Yours sincerely
Percy.

P. S. Messrs. Baker, Palmer, Gair &c who are on board with me beg I will present their Comp^ts.—

III

To the Duke of Northumberland

Boston, July 5, 1774.

My dearest Father:

AS I am certain you will be anxious to hear from me, I take the earliest opportunity after my arrival, of acquainting

---

him sensitive to criticism of either; and readers of Boswell will recall an amusing account of a quarrel between Dr. Percy and Johnson at a dinner, April 12, 1778. The last years of his life were spent in Ireland as bishop of Dromore.

you that I am here & in good health.¹ You will perceive by the date of this (for we only came about an hour ago) that we have had a very bad passage. I have the misfortune, for I must think it so, of commanding the camp here. The people, by all accounts, are extremely violent & wrong headed, so much so that I fear we shall be obliged to come to extremities. . . . I am in a complete scene of confusion, as we are to land & encamp directly. Adieu, my dearest Father, & be assured, I ever remain

Your dutiful son,
Percy.

I beg my best duty to my mother, to whom I shall write in a day or two.

IV

To the Duke of Northumberland

Camp at Boston, July 27, 1774.

My dearest Father:

AS I find a ship is likely to sail to-morrow for England, I cannot help taking this opportunity for letting you hear from me. I am, I thank God, in perfect health, tho' I was threatened with the gout for the first fortnight after my arri-

---

[1] *Camp at Boston, July* 5th, 1774. I DO certify that His Majesty's Fifth Regiment of Foot embarked on board the Symmetry, Father's Good Will, Alicia, and Henry, transports, on the 7th of May last, at the Cove of Cork, complete according to the establishment, excepting Lieut. Francia, Lord Rawdon, and Ensign Henry King, ordered to join, but not then joined . . . and disembarked this evening at Boston in N. America, complete, wanting the above officers, and Lieut. and Quarter Master Robert Palmer, who died in the passage on the 9th of June, 1774.

val. As Genl. Gage received orders to remain at Salem, I have been left commanding officer of the camp, ever since my first coming here (except for about a week). The General has done Col. Pigott & me the honor of appointing us to act as Brigadiers, a compliment always paid to Col^s. in the field. However, we are both obliged to lay in camp. As my mother has lately chose to collect views, I have the pleasure of enclosing for her two cards, which when put together as marked on the back, exhibit a most perfect view of the town of Boston,—together with a third, which is a view of our camp.[1] I hope they will be agreable to her, as they are very exact. The people here talk much & do little; but nothing, I am sure, will ever reestablish peace & quiet in this country, except steadiness & perseverance on the part of Administration. A change of Administration or measures would be, at this instant, the most fatal thing in the world to this province, & All America in general, for it would be adding fresh fuel to that flame which the frequent changes in both were the origin of. Genl. Gage has done his duty with great coolness & firmness, & if Administration does not support him, they never again deserve to be well served. The people in this part of the country are in general made up of rashness & timidity. Quick & violent in their determinations, they are fearful in the execution of them (unless, indeed, they are quite certain of meeting little or no opposition, & then, like all other cowards, they are cruel and tyrannical). To hear them talk, you would imagine that they would attack us & demolish us every night;

---

[1] *Several views of Boston, showing the camp, still exist, although few if any were executed as early as July. Possibly Percy refers to a drawing. Mrs. Ruthy Andrews was then living in the town, and her pen-and-ink landscapes excited his admiration. (Massachusetts Historical Society Proceedings, July, 1865, page 403.)*

& yet, whenever we appear, they are frightened out of their wits. They begin to feel a little the effects of the Port Bill,[1] & were they not supported by the other Colonies, must before this have submitted. One thing I will be bold to say, which is, that till you make their Committees of Correspondence and Congress[es] with the other Colonies high treason, & try them for it in England, you never must expect perfect obedience & submission from this to the Mother Country. I am sorry to say that no body of men in this Province are so extremely injurious to the peace & tranquility of it as the clergy. They preach up sedition openly from their pulpits. (Nay, some of them have gone so far as absolutely to refuse the sacrament to the communicants till they have signed a paper of the most seditious kind, which they have denominated the Solemn League and Covenant). So much with respect to the inhabitants. As for a description of the country and its productions, I must defer that till another letter. With regard to the climate, it is ten times more inconstant than in England, for I have been in the Torrid & Frigid Zone frequently in the space of 24 hours. At some times, so hot as scarce to bear my shirt, at others so cold that an additional blanket was scarcely sufficient. I am afraid that you will hardly be able to read this letter, but the ship sails early tomorrow, & I did not know anything of it till eleven this night; & you are sensible that my

---

[1] *The Boston Port Bill became a law March* 31, 1774, *and its provisions went into effect on the first of June. It made Salem the seat of government, Marblehead the port of entry, and closed Boston's trade by sea during the King's pleasure.*

Grey Cooper, one of Percy's correspondents, said: "*This Bill, Sir, I look upon to be the act of a father chastising his son on one line, and restoring the trade and peace of America on the other, and therefore I highly approve of the measure.*" (*Force's American Archives*, 4*th series, vol. i., column* 52.)

PERCY LETTERS

eyes do not allow me in general to ink by candle light. . . .
Opportunities of writing to England are very few & uncertain. I beg you will present the enclosed card with my duty to my mother, as also my love to my brother, if he is with you; & be assured that I am, & ever shall remain, your most dutiful & most affectionate son

PERCY.

V

To HENRY REVELEY,[1] *Esq., Peckham, Surrey.*

Camp at Boston, Aug. 8, 1774.

. . . THIS is the most beautiful country I ever saw in my life, & if the people were only like it, we shd do very well. Everything, however, is as yet quiet, but they threaten much. Not that I believe they dare act. As Gen. Gage is obliged by orders to reside at Salem, I have the honour of

---

[1] *In Hodgson's Northumberland, part* 2, *vol. ii.* (1832), *page* 70, *and in Burke's Commoners (edition of* 1836), *vol. iii., pages* 132, 133, *will be found accounts of the Reveley family.*

William Reveley of Newton Underwood, Northumberland, later of Newby Wiske, born in 1662.	=	Margery, daughter of Robert Willey of Newby Wiske, county York.				
Willey Reveley = Rachel Neale.		George Reveley = Elizabeth Tucker.		Philadelphia Reveley, born in 1688.	=	Langdale Smithson, son of Sir Hugh Smithson, Bart.
Henry Reveley, born 1718, died 1800, unmarried.		HENRY REVELEY born 1737, died 1798. Connoisseur in music and art.	= Jane Champion de Crespigny.	Sir Hugh Smithson, 1st Duke of Northumberland.	=	Lady Elizabeth Seymour, heiress of the Percies.
		Hugh, etc.		HUGH, EARL PERCY, *born* 1742.		

commanding the Troops encamped here, wh consist of the 4th, 5th, 23^d, 38th, & 43^d Reg^{ts}, besides 3 co^s of artillery, who have with them 4, 12-pounders 12, 6-pounders & 4 howitzers. And the Genl has appointed Col. Pigott & myself to act as Brigadier Gen^{ls}.[1] . . . We have days here full as hot as Spain. . . . But our climate is horribly inconstant, for we have it sometimes very cold. But I think ever since we landed, it has in general been full as hot as the South of France.

The people here are a set of sly, artful, hypocritical rascalls, cruel, & cowards. I must own I cannot but despise them compleately. . . . God knows when I shall return, for I do not see the least prospect of any alteration in matters here as yet, & whilst things continue in their present situation, I cannot stir. . . .

Y^r aff. cousin & sincere friend
PERCY.

VI

To the DUKE OF NORTHUMBERLAND

Camp at Boston, Aug. 15, 1774.

My dearest Father:

AS I find the Scarborough has not yet sailed . . . tho' I have written to my mother by the same ship . . . our opportunities of conveying letters to Europe from this place are so few & so precious, that whenever there is a good &

---

[1] Lord Percy discusses at some length his rank in the army.

PERCY LETTERS

safe one, I shall never let you fail to hear from me. The affairs of this country remain in precisely the same situation as when I did myself the pleasure of writing to you on the 27th of last month.... & as in that letter I attempted to give you some account of the inhabitants, I shall now endeavor to do the same with regard to the country.

And, I assure you, it requires a far abler pen than mine to describe its different beauties. It is, as far at least as I have been round this town, most delightfully varied. The hills, rising from the valleys by gradual & gentle ascents, interspersed everywhere with trees, give it a most agreable appearance. Nor do the small lakes of water with which the country abounds, contribute little towards the richness of the scene. In short, it has everywhere the appearance of a Park finely laid out. Mr. Browne here wd be useless. Nature has, in this part of the world, taken upon herself his employment, & dressed the ground in a manner that no art can ever equal. The trees in this country consist chiefly of the black & white oak, the elm, a species of the sycamore (wh they call the button tree), & the locust tree. This last is of the acacia kind, but remarkably hardy, & as it grows among the crevices of the rocks, & is not so brittle as the acacia itself, I shd think it wd do very well in some parts of Hulne Park [1]: especially as neither winds, frost, nor snow affect it.

What has struck me here very much is that the elder, wh in Eng^d grows to be a tree, never can in this country be made to exceed the size of a common shrub, much about the size of our English quick hedges. The boughs of all the

---

[1] *The park at Alnwick contains within its present bounds the domains of two ancient religious houses: Alnwick Abbey, founded in* 1147, *and Hulne Priory, dating from* 1240.

trees here hang very much in the manner of our weeping willow, wh gives them a very picturesque appearance. This I can account for no way, unless it is owing to the quantity of snow that lays on them all winter, & wh, by giving them that bend when they are young, may occasion them to retain that drooping form ever afterwards: and this I am the more apt to believe, as I am informed that the same trees more to the Southward have it not.

But, however beautiful the outward appearance of this country may be, it is amply made up for by the poverty of the soil, wh I rather believe is owing to the ground's being exhausted by constant crops, without manure, than to any natural defect in the soil itself. Let what will be the reason, this Province now only produces miserable crops of Rye, worse of Oats, & a great quantity of Indian corn; which last article is of the greatest service to the country, as it is the food of the people, their cattle of all kinds, & their fowls. The oxen are remarkably large & fine, & these they make use of for every kind of draught. I cannot, however, say much for their horses, wh in general, are a good deal like the German ones. There are, nevertheless, some that are of a better sort, but then they ask an immoderate price for them. I believe I have bought one of the handsomest in this country; & you will be surprised to hear that I was forced to give 450£ for him; but not so much so, when I inform you that the above sum does not amount to more than 45£ sterling. However, this is dear enough for a horse that is barely 3 yrs old.

I have also got some tolerable chaise-horses from N. Y., for there were none good eno' in this country. But what I feel myself the most comfortable in acquiring, is a good house[1] to dine in (for we are all obliged to remain at other times & sleep in camp). By this convenience I am enabled to ask the officers of the Line, & occasionally the Gentlemen of the country, to dine with me;[2] & as I have the command of the Troops here, I have always a table of 12 covers every day. This, tho' very expensive, is however very necessary. It is surprising to think how much dearer everything is here than in Europe, nay, even than in London. And they now begin to ask double what they did on our first arrival, owing to the great quantities that are consumed by such a no. of Troops.

I have now quite a little army under my command, 5 Reg^{ts} & 22 pieces of cannon, with a proper no. of the Royal Corps of Artillery to work them.

I shd imagine, however, from some informations wh I have rec^d that it will be necessary to detach a Brigade up farther into the country; for I understand the people are beginning to be a little troublesome there. As I cannot say this is a business I very much admire, I hope it will not be my fate to be ordered up with them. I wait, however, for the Governor's determination on this subject. . . . Be that as it may, I am resolved cheerfully to do my duty as long as ever I continue in the service.[3] . . .

---

[1] *This was no doubt an old-fashioned wooden house, formerly occupied by Sir Francis Bernard. It stood in a pleasant garden at the northerly corner of Winter and Tremont (then Common) streets. John Andrews in a letter dated August* 31, 1774, *said: " His Excellency . . . proceeded to Earl Piercy's, who occupies a house at the head of Winter Street." (Massachusetts Historical Society Proceedings, July,* 1865, *page* 350.)

[2] *" George and I come in sometimes for a good dinner among the great people, and are particularly indebted to Lord Percy and General Clinton." (Memoir and Letters of W. G. Evelyn, edited by Scull, page* 66.)

[3] *Percy's attitude toward the Administration in England probably deferred the advancement to which his military services and social position seemed to entitle him.*

PERCY LETTERS

VII

To GENERAL HARVEY (?)

Camp at Boston, Aug. 21, 1774.

... OUR affairs here seem to be still in the same state. It is true, we have at last got the New Act,[1] & twenty-six of the new Council have accepted & are sworn in; but for my own part, I doubt whether they will be more active than the old ones. Such a set of timid creatures I never did see. Those of the new Council that live at any distance from town have remained here ever since they took the oaths, & are, I am told, afraid to go home again.

As for the opposite party, they are arming & exercising all over the country. Yet I am still convinced that nothing but either drunkenness or madness can force (?) them to molest us. If, however, they once begin, I fear there will be some bloodshed.

Their method of eluding that part of the Act wh relates to the town meetings is strongly characteristic of the people. They say that since the town meetings are forbid by the Act, they shall not hold them, but as they do not see any mention made of county meetings, they shall hold *them* for the future. They, therefore, go a mile out of Town, do just the same business there they formerly did in Boston, call it a county meeting, & so elude the Act.

---

[1] *The Regulation Acts, passed in April, were received by Governor Gage in August, and when put in force, swept away the rights of Massachusetts under the charter. Councillors, judges, and sheriffs ceased to derive authority from the people; town meetings were deprived of their influence; and power to quarter troops on the towns permitted the governor to penetrate every house with his soldiers.*

PERCY LETTERS

In short, I am certain that it will require a great length of time, much steadiness, and many troops, to reestablish good order & government. . . . I plainly foresee that there is not a new councillor or magistrate who will dare to act without at least a reg^t at his heels, & it is not quite clear to me that he will even act then, as he ought to do.

Our force is much increased since I last wrote. . . . 2 co^s of the 64th are encamped at Danvers, to cover the Governor's house where he resides. The 59th Reg^t are encamped at Salem, to cover & protect the meetings of the new Council. The remaining co^s of the 64th are at Castle William, to wh place most of the powder & other stores belonging to the artillery are removed from N. Y. Besides wh, I have under my command, the 4th, 5th, 38th & 43^d Reg^{ts}, together with 22 pieces of cannon & 3 co^s of artillery encamped on the Common, & the Welsh Fusileers encamped on the Fort Hill at Boston. The Govr, however, talks of sending a Brigade out of this n^o. up into the country, to protect the magistrates at a distance. I expect him here in a few days, when I fancy this matter will be settled.

Our desertion is now greatly decreased. We have lost only one man for upwards of a fortnight. Indeed, I send out such frequent patrols & parties, that they must be the most fortunate men on earth to escape them.

Our weather here is extremely hot. . . . Notwithstanding this, we are remarkably healthy. Not a single man has died in this camp since our arrival.

The Delegates from this Province[1] are set out to meet the

---

[1] *Samuel Adams, John Adams, Thomas Cushing,* and *Robert Treat Paine* represented Massachusetts on the opening day of Congress at 'the Carpenter's Hall,' September 5, 1774.

Genl Congress at Phila. They talk much of non-importation, & an agreement between all the Colonies. If this shd really be the case, I hope Gt. Britain will not allow them to trade with anybody else. I flatter myself, however, that instead of agreeing to anything they will all go by the ears together at this Congress. If they don't, there will be more work cut out for Administration in Am. than perhaps they are aware of.[1]
Adieu, my dear General ——

VIII

To the DUKE OF NORTHUMBERLAND

Camp at Boston, Sept. 12, 1774.

My dearest Father:

... I HAVE great reason to believe that letters sent by the Post are opened & often stop^t.... Things here are now drawing to a crisis every day. The People here openly oppose the New Acts. They have taken up arms in almost every part of this Province, & have drove in the Govr & most of the Council. The few that remain in the country, they have not only obliged to resign, but to take up arms with them. A few days ago, they mustered about 7000 men at Worcester, to wh place they have conveyed about 20 pieces of cannon.

In short, this country is now in as open a state of rebellion as Scotland was in the year '45.

The General's great lenity and moderation serve only to

---

[1] *This paragraph, with several others, appears in Mr. Porter's "The Beginning of the Revolution," a chapter in Winsor's Memorial History of Boston, vol. iii.* (1881), *pages* 56, 57.

make them more daring & insolent. It is astonishing with what discretion & prudence he behaves himself. He has given them every proof that his utmost wish is to restore peace & tranquillity without coming to violent measures. But this behavior they term timidity, & fancy that the troops are unable to act against them, an error wh some time or other they will find out to their cost. He has given orders for fortifying the town, that His Majesty's troops & peaceful subjects may at least be protected from the insults of a mad & outrageous rabble; & I fancy, means to act entirely on the defensive. We have this day begun upon the works. . . .

What makes an insurrection here always more formidable than in other places, is that there is a law of this Province, wh obliges every inhabitant to be furnished with a firelock, bayonet, & pretty considerable quantity of ammunition. Besides wh, every township is obliged by the same law to have a large magazine of all kinds of military stores.

They are, moreover, trained four times in each year, so that they do not make a despicable *appearance* as soldiers, tho' they were never yet known to behave themselves even decently in the field. . . . The Genl has not yet molested them in the least. They have even free access to and from this town, tho' armed with firelocks, provided they only come in small n^{os}. . . . You will be able to judge from the acc't I have given you what a pretty state things are in here. Besides wh, as they will neither suffer any courts to sit or magistrates to act, there is a total suspension of all Law and Justice. . . . I have lately not been well. . . . My complaint was bilious, a very common distemper in this country. . . .

PERCY LETTERS

IX

To . . . . . .

$Oct.$ 10, 74.

AS an extraord'y public'n has appeared in a newspaper of this town, wholly subversive of all mil'y obed & discipline, I cannot help thinking it my duty to send you the particulars of that transaction. . . . When, to the astonishment of everybody, the whole affair appeared in the Massa^{tts} Spy . . . one wd really think that the spirit of the inhab^s had got amongst the officers, for there is almost every day some complaint or other from the different commanding officers, owing to a certain unwillingness wh the young men in gen^l discover to proper obed & discipline.[1]

---

[1] *The Massachusetts Spy of September 29th printed a communication, apparently written by an officer in Lord Percy's regiment; this notice, probably referred to above, bears the heading*:

Proceedings of a regimental court martial, held in his Majesty's 5th regiment of foot, by order of the commanding officer; of which Capt. Jackson, was president, Lieut. Cox, Lieut. Croker, Ensign Patrick, and Ensign King, members.

The court sat on the 5th of September, 1774, to try William Fanthrop for being drunk when on piquet and for opposing the corporal who was ordered to take away his arms. He was declared guilty and sentenced to receive two hundred lashes. The commanding officer considered the sentence inadequate and rather than have it read before the men ordered Fanthrop's release. The communication, after making these facts public, concludes: " *How are military gentlemen now-a-days to act? their honour slighted, and their characters injured, by tyrannical commanders! Can officers do their duty with that spirit, becoming their character, when treated by their commanders in such an infamous manner? Were it not for the present unsettled state of this country, and serving their King, what officer would serve in a regiment to be thus scandalously abused?* "

PERCY LETTERS

X

To the Rev. THOMAS PERCY

Camp at Boston, Octr. 27th. 1774.

HOW shall I thank my good D^{r}. Percy for the Letters He has been so kind as to write to me, or what return can I make Him for the Entertainment they have given me? As I find it is impossible, I'll give it up handsomely at once, & think [no] more of it.

Our affairs here are in the most Critical Situation imaginable; Nothing less than the total loss or Conquest of the Colonies must be the End of it. Either indeed is disagreable, but one or the other is now absolutely necessary.

We have got together a clever little Army here 8 Reg^{ts} of Infantry besides two which are daily expected, together with a pretty small train of Artillery. However many more will be wanted next Spring. You may judge a little of the temper of the People by an Address which I have enclosed to my Mother. Our Weather here is charming; It was so warm yesterday & is again so warm to day that I am obliged to sit with all my Windows open. Nay even this morning when I went to visit the Out-Posts at daybreak it was quite mild & pleasant. But we must soon expect to change this Weather for Frost & Snow; for I am told the transition from Summer to Winter is very sudden in this Climate.

Do let me know in your next, how my Brother does, & what He is about. I have not received one Letter from Him for upwards of a twelvemonth, tho' I have frequently wrote to Him.

PERCY LETTERS

Adieu My Dear Doctor make my Comp^ts. agreable to your Family & believe me to be
                    Your sincere Friend
                                PERCY.
To
    The Rev^d. D^r. PERCY.

XI

To GENERAL HARVEY (?)

Nov. 1, 1774.
My dear GEN^L.

THINGS here grow more & more serious every day. The Prov^l Congress at Camb have now come to resolutions wh must be attended with fatal consequences to this country. They have voted an army of observation of 15000 men, & have appointed a com of 15, who are to have the conduct & management of the affairs of this Province; but they are particularly to take care that proper magazines are formed . . . & that their army is supplied with everything proper for carrying on a war.

They have chose Col. Ward, Col. Preble, & Col. Pomeroy, Gen^ls to command this army, wh is to be divided for the winter into 3 corps: one at Charlestown, wh is just on the other side of the harbor from Boston, one at Roxbury, wh is just at the opposite end of the neck from Boston; & one at Cambridge, wh is about 6 m. distant, & wh last place is to be Headquarters.

PERCY LETTERS

It was for a long time debated in their councils whether they shd not form an encampment immediately, on some high ground just above Roxbury, & within random shot of our lines: but as the season was so far advanced, the other plan was thot more advisable. As they only came to this resol^n on the 29th of last month, they have not as yet assembled. If they really shd do so, I take it for granted the Genl will think it necessary to deprive them of part of their quarters, at least, by burning Charlestown & Roxbury directly.

These resol^s they have kept private, for pretty good & substantial reasons, tho' those they have ventured to publish are not very moderate, as you may see by the enclosed newspaper.[1]

Our little army is now all collected here, together with Gen. Haldimand & the Am. Staff. We still remain encamped, nor, indeed, have we much prospect of getting into quarters for near a month, as there has been the greatest difficulty in procuring proper places to convert into barracks; but as the weather still continues fine, the men have not as yet suffered by it.

Gen. Gage (by some conversation I have lately had with him on that subject) will, I fancy, be very earnest in his solicitations for more troops, & ind[eed] they will be absolutely wanted if we are to move into the country next spring, to enforce the New Acts. For, as this place is the fountain from whence spring all their mad & treasonable resolves & actions, it will be nec'y to leave a very large corps here, to

---

[1] *General Harvey wrote to Percy in April of the year following: "The resolves of the Prov^l Congress are curious. Let Eng^d keep steady, & their resolves & madness must vanish. How far Franklyn may electrify, I can't tell, but a steady, cool, and conciliatory perseverance will even cool the fiery Doctor."*

keep the town in order & protect the friends of Gov^t. Besides wh, two other corps will be wanted to cover the flanks of the main body that attempts to march into the country.

Col. Jones, who is arrived from Quebeck with the (52^d) Reg^t, has bro't an offer to the Genl of 5000 Canadians & 1200 Indians.

XII

To the Rev. THOMAS PERCY

Boston, Novr. 25th. 1774.

Dear D^R.

BY some unfortunate Accident, I dont get my News-Papers for above a Month after everybody else, for example my latest Papers are of the 9th of Sept^r. & we have received Papers as late as the 15th. of Octr. This I fancy must be owing to their sending them to some Coffee House to proceed by Ships, who never sail for a Month so soon as they say they will. Whereas it will be a much more safe & speedy method to divide them into three or four Parcells, & send them out by the Pacquet which sails from Falmouth. If therefore they are directed to me here & sent the first Wednesday in every Month to the Genl. Post Office, they will come both quicker & safer. Our Winter is now come on here, but I cannot say as yet I find it colder than in England. We have had little or no Snow, but a great deal of Rain, & violent Gales of Wind. However we luckily got into Winter Quarters about a week ago, before it came on.

Our Affairs here still continue in the same Posture; The Provincial Congress I find met again yesterday, & I am informed they mean to proceed to the choice of a new Gov'. They have already raised an Army, seized the Publick Money, & have taken on themselves all the Powers of Government. I really begin now to think that it will come to Blows at last; For They are most amazingly encouraged by our having done nothing as yet.

In short they have now got to such lengths that nothing can secure the Colonies to the Mother Country, but the Conquest of them. The People here are the most designing, Artfull Villains in the World. They have not the least Idea of either Religion or Morality. Nor have they the least Scruple of taking the most solemn Oath on any Matter that can assist their Purpose, tho' they know the direct contrary can be clearly & evidently proved in half an Hour.

Of this We have had several Instances. May I beg you will be so kind as to send me out Here the following Books. The new Edition of Manstein's Memoirs of Russia — History of the War in America by Mante[1] — & Avis d'une Mère à un fils par la Marquise de Lambert — I need not make any excuses to you for giving you this trouble as I know you are always ready to assist your Friends. I still continue to enjoy my health perfectly. The constant exercise which my Duty obliges me to take in visiting all the Out-Posts every other morning about day break together with the morning Air, contributes not a little to keep me in Health. I forgot amongst the List of Books to desire you to send me Les Memoires de Mons'. de Feuquières. You will

---

[1] *Thomas Mante's History of the French and Indian War.*

be so good as to send them off as soon as you get any of them as I mean them chiefly for my Winter's Amusement. Adieu Dear D^r. make my Comp^{ts}. agreable to all your Family & believe me to be
Your sincere Friend
PERCY.

P. S. I have sent you enclosed a Ridicule upon the Genl. Congress.
To
The Rev^d. D^r. PERCY.

XIII

To HENRY REVELEY, Esq.

Boston, Dec. 6, 1774.

Dear REVELEY:

... You see I am not yet dead, though the Morning Chronicle has been so good as to kill me: nor indeed, in the way of dying, for I never enjoyed my health better. The *Scarborough* Man of War returned to us last Saturday from Eng. What orders she has brought, nobody knows. Everything is kept quite secret.

The *Asia* came in here, also, on Monday, but waits for the spring tides to get up. The *Somerset* and the *Boyne* are not yet arrived, but we expect them every day. This Reinforcement gives great spirits, as you may imagine, to the Friends of Government, & has frightened the Sons of Liberty (as they call themselves) confoundedly.

PERCY LETTERS

However, as nothing has been done in consequence of the arrival of these ships, they begin to feel Bold again.'....

Y^r sincere Friend &c.
PERCY.

XIV

To GREY COOPER,[2] Esq.

GREY COOPER, Esq.   [*After December* 13, 1774.]

SIR: I shd not think of troubling you... had not an extrad'y event taken place at Portsmouth, in N. H. On Monday or Tuesday last, M^r. Paul Revere (a person who is employed by the Com of Correspondence, here, as a messenger) arrived at Portsmth with a letter from the Com here to those of that place, on the receipt of wh circular letters were wrote to all the neighboring towns; & an armed body of 400 or 500 men marched the next day into the town of Portsmouth, and proceeded from thence to the fort near Newcastle, at the entrance of the harbor, wh was garrisoned by only a Capt. and 4 or 5 gunners. This fort they attacked and carried, from whence they have removed upwards of 100 barrels of powder, 1500 stand of small arms, and several pieces of light cannon, from 3 to 12 pounders, to the am't (as I am informed) of 30 or upwards. With this prize they marched afterwards to Exeter, a

---

[1] *A reference to his rank in the army follows.*

[2] *Grey Cooper (calling himself " Sir Grey Cooper, Bart.," after* 1775) *was at this time joint Secretary of the Treasury, an able financier and administrator who held the office until* 1782. *He died July* 30, 1801, *at the age of seventy-five years.*

PERCY LETTERS

town about 16 miles distant from Portsm, where they have secured them under a strong guard.[1]

What is the most extraordy in this event is, that notwithstanding the Capt fired at them, both with some field pieces and small arms, nobody was either killed or wounded. They kept the Capt and his men prisoners till they had removed everything, and then set them at liberty.

By this, and what has lately happened at R. I., you will see how universal this Spirit is,[2] and to what a length it has got, and therefore how nec'y to crush it before it is too late. . . . A ship sails tomorrow for Glasgow.

XV

To General Harvey[3]

Boston, Feb. 9, '75.

. . . Things are in a strange unsettled state here. The leaders undoubtedly grow more desperate as they see less hopes of escaping, and do all they can to drive the others to extremi-

---

[1] *Substantially the same story appears in Force's American Archives, 4th series, vol. i., column 1053. Revere was sent December 12th to warn the Portsmouth patriots that two British ships had sailed from Boston to seize the powder at Fort William and Mary.*

[2] *Writing to his father January 25, 1775, Lord Percy says: "Both parties here are waiting impatiently for the determinations on your side of the Atlantick. If Gt Britain relaxes in the least, adieu to the colonies. They will be lost forever." The Duke, never in sympathy with the war, obtained, December 5, 1774, an order permitting General Gage to send his son to England. This offer Lord Percy declined because his duty lay with the army in America. (See De Fonblanque's Annals of the House of Percy, where this letter is mentioned.)*

[3] *Edward Harvey, lieutenant-general in 1772, member of Parliament for Harwich, and "governor of the town and isle of Portsmouth and South Sea Castle," died March 27, 1778. (Gentleman's Magazine for 1778, page 142.)*

ties —— We are waiting with impatience the determinations and orders from yr side of the water. Whatever they are, I hope they will be pointed and effectual ones; for you left so many loopholes in the last acts you passed, that it was found not possible to enforce them.'....

XVI

To the Rev. THOMAS PERCY

Boston, Ap^l. 8th. 1775.

Dear D^R.

THO' I have wrote so lately both to my Father & Mother, yet I always take every opportunity of letting some of you at North^d. House hear from me. Things now every day begin to grow more & more serious; A Vessel is arrived by accident here that has brought us a Newspaper in which we have the joint Address of the two Houses of Parliament to His Majesty; this has convinced the Rebels (for we may now legally call them so) that there is no hopes for them but by submitting to Parliament; they have therefore begun seriously to form their Army & have already appointed all the Staff. They are every day in greater Numbers evacuating this Town & have proposed in Congress, either to set it on Fire & attack the troops before a reinforcement comes, or to endeavour to starve us. Which they mean to adopt, time only can show. The Genl. however has received no Acc^t. whatever from Europe, so that [on] our side no steps of any kind can be taken as yet.

[1] *A reference to the conduct of two company officers follows.*

PERCY LETTERS

The Weather here for the last three weeks has been cold & disagreable, a kind of second Winter, however as this day is remarkably warm & fine I flatter myself our good Weather is now beginning. Thank God, I still continue to enjoy my health perfectly & have very much surprised the Inhabitants here by going constantly all Winter with my bosom open without a Great Coat. They own however that this was a remarkably mild Winter. I think I have felt it colder in England.

Adieu my Dear D^r. Make my Duty agreable to My Father & Mother & be assured I ever am

Your sincere Friend
Percy.

XVII

To Governor Gage *of Massachusetts*

(Official Account of the Retreat from Lexington)

Boston, 20 *April*, 1775.

S^R,—

IN obedience to your Excell^s orders I marched yesterday morning at 9 o'clk, with the first Brigade and 2 Fieldpieces, in order to cover the retreat of the Grenadiers & Light Infy, on their return from The Expedition to Concord.[1]

---

[1] *Percy marched through Brookline, and it is the tradition that he was taunted with verses from Chevy Chase. Curiously enough, Horace Walpole, on hearing of the encounter, wrote to Sir Horace Mann from Strawberry Hill, June 5th:*

So here is this fatal war commenced!
The child that is unborn shall rue
The hunting of that day!

As all the houses were shut up, & there was not the appearance of a single inhabitant, I could get no intelligence concerning them till I had passed Menotomy, when I was informed that the Rebels had attacked His Majesty's Troops, who were retiring, overpowered by numbers, greatly exhausted & fatigued, & having expended almost all their ammunition. And about 2 o'clk I met them retiring through the Town of Lexington.

I immediately ordered the 2 field-pieces to fire at the Rebels, and drew up the Brigade on a height. The shot from the cannon had the desired effect, & stopped the Rebels for a little time, who immediately dispersed, & endeavoured to surround us, being very numerous. As it began now to grow pretty late, & we had 15 miles to retire, & only our 36 rounds, I ordered the Grenadiers and Lgt Infy to move off first, & covered them with my Brigade, sending out very strong flanking parties, wh were absolutely necessary, as there was not a stone-wall, or house, though before in appearance evacuated, from whence the Rebels did not fire upon us.

As soon as they saw us begin to retire, they pressed very much upon our rear-guard, which for that reason I relieved every now & then. In this manner we retired for 15 miles under an incessant fire all round us, till we arrived at Charlestown, between 7 & 8 in the even, very much fatigued with a march of above 30 miles, & having expended almost all our ammunition.

We had the misfortune of losing a good many men in the retreat, tho' nothing like the number wh, from many circumstances, I have reason to believe were killed of the Rebels.

His Majesty's Troops during the whole of the affair be-

PERCY LETTERS

haved with their usual intrepidity & spirit. Nor were they a little exasperated at the cruelty and barbarity of the Rebels, who scalped & cut off the ears of some of the wounded men who fell into their hands.[1]

I am, &c
   Signed PERCY
       Acting Brig Gen.

To the Honble *Gov*^R GAGE

---

[1] *The same report, indorsed* "*In the Hon*^{ble} *Gov*^r *Gage's* (*No.* 28) *of April,* 1775," *is in the* P. R. O. *America and West Indies, vol.* 130; *reprinted Massachusetts Historical Society Proceedings, May,* 1876, *page* 349.

This version differs slightly from another found at Alnwick Castle, copied in part by Mr. Porter, with his comment: "*Evidently a rough draft copy of his report to Gen. Gage.*"

                        Apr 20, '75.
SIR:

AT Menotomy, I was informed by a person whom I met that there had been a skirmish between his Maj's troops & the rebels at Lexⁿ, & that they were still engaged. On this, I immediately pressed on, & in less than 2 miles we heard the firing very distinctly. About this time (wh was between 1 and 2 o'clk in the aftⁿ) I met with L^t. Gould of the King's Own Reg, who was wounded, & who informed me that the Gren^s & L[ight] I[nfantry] had been attacked by the rebels about daybreak, & were retiring, having expended most of their ammunition: & in about a quarter of an hour I met them retiring thro' Lexⁿ. I immed^{ly} ordered the two field pieces to fire at the Rebels. . . . The shot from the cannon had the desired effect. . . . In this manner we retired for 15 m. under an incessant fire all round us, till we arrived at Cha^stown, wh road I chose to take, lest the rebels shd have taken up the bridge at Cambridge (wh I find was actually the case), & also as the country was more open & the road shorter. During the whole of our retreat, the rebels endeavored to annoy us by concealing themselves behind stone walls & within houses, & firing straggling shot at us from thence; nor did I during the whole time perceive any body of them drawn up together, exc. near Cambr, just as we turned down towards Cha^stown, who dispersed on a cannon shot being fired at them, & came down to attack our right flank in the same straggling manner the rest had done before. . . . In obed. to Y^r Excellency's command, I have drawn up the above state^t of the affair. . . .

               & I am &c ——

PERCY LETTERS

XVIII

To General Harvey

(Part of an unofficial account of the retreat from Lexington)

Ap[l] 20, 1775. *Boston.*

... I THEREFORE pressed on to [the] relief [of the British troops] as fast as good order & not blowing the men would allow. ... The rebels were in great no[s]., the whole country having collected for 20 m around. ... I ordered the Gren[adier]s & L[ight] I[nfantry] to move off, covering them with my Brig[ade], & detaching strong flanking parties wh was absolutely nec'y, as the whole country we had to retire thro' was cov[d] with stone walls, & was besides a very hilly, stony country. In this manner, we retired for 15 m under an incessant fire, wh like a moving circle surrounded & fol[d] us wherever we went, till we arrived at Charlestown at 8 in the ev'g, ... & having expended almost every cartridge. You will easily conceive that in such a retreat, harassed as we were on all sides, it was impossible not to lose a good many men.

The following is an acct of them: 65 k[illed], 157 w[ounded], & 21 m[issing], besides 1 offi[r] k[illed], 15 w[ounded], & 2 w[ounded] & taken prisoners. ... During the whole affair the Rebels attacked us in a very scattered, irregular manner, but with perseverance & resolution, nor did they ever dare to form into any regular body. Indeed, they knew too well what was proper, to do so.

Whoever looks upon them as an irregular mob, will find

himself much mistaken. They have men amongst them who know very well what they are about, having been employed as Rangers agst the Indians & Canadians, & this country being much cov^d w. wood, and hilly, is very advantageous for their method of fighting.

Nor are several of their men void of a spirit of enthusiasm, as we experienced yesterday, for many of them concealed themselves in houses, & advanced within 10 yds. to fire at me & other officers, tho' they were morally certain of being put to death themselves in an instant.

You may depend upon it, that as the Rebels have now had time to prepare, they are determined to go thro' with it, nor will the insurrection here turn out so despicable as it is perhaps imagined at home. <u>For my part, I never believed, I confess, that they wd have attacked the King's troops, or have had the perseverance I found in them yesterday.</u>

I have myself fortunately escaped very well, having only had a horse shot. Poor Lt.-Cols Smith & Barnard, are both wounded, but not badly.'. . .

---

[1] *Two letters which follow refer to Lord Percy's part in the affair:*

General GAGE to Lord DARTMOUTH:

L^D Percy arrived opportunely to their assistance, his Brigade & 2 p[iece]s of cannon, & notwithstanding a continual skirmish for the space of 15 m[ile]s, receiving Fire from every hill, fence, house, barn, &c, his Lordship kept the enemy off, & bro't the Troops to Cha^{s}town, from whence they were ferried over to Boston.

Too much praise cannot be given to Ld Percy for his remarkable activity & conduct during the whole day.

      Killed 62
      Wound^d 157
      Missing 24

Lord DRUMMOND to [Lord DARTMOUTH]:

[1775, *June* 9.] 10 *o'clock evening. Whitehall.*

HAS just seen a letter dated Boston 21 April from a gentleman of some importance who has arrived there from Salem which place he quitted on account of the affair of the 19th;

PERCY LETTERS

XIX

To the DUKE OF NORTHUMBERLAND[1]

Boston, 20 *Ap^l* [1775].

I WAS ordered out yesterday morning to cover the retreat of the Grenadiers and Lgt Infy, who had been sent upon an exped^n into the country.[2] I had with me my Brigade [and] 2 p[iece]s of cannon. We met them at a Town about 15 m[ile]s off, sharply attacked & surrounded by the Rebels, having fired away almost all their ammunition. I had the happiness, however, of saving them from inevitable destruction, & arrived with them at Chastown, opposite Boston, ab^t 8 o'clk last night, not, however, without the loss of a great many, having been under an incessant fire for 15 m[ile]s.

The Rebels, however, have suffered much more than the King's Troops. I have not [myself] rec^d even the least scratch, so I beg you will not [either of you] be uneasy on my account. There can now surely be no doubt of their being in open Re-

---

he states that the retreat by Lord Percy was deemed a piece of masterly officership in bringing off his men with so little loss through a severe and incessant fire for twenty miles; killed, wounded and missing between 80 and 100 including many officers. The provincials were endeavouring to cut off communication between the town and country and they were computed at 20,000. Lord Percy is in good health at General Gage's house.
Autograph letter signed. 3 quarto pages.
Endorsed: — Ld Drummond 9th June 1775. Intelligence from Boston.
(*From 14th report of the Royal Commission on Historical Manuscripts, Appendix, part x., page* 312 — *Dartmouth MSS., vol. ii.*)

[1] *This letter is printed in De Fonblanque's Annals of the House of Percy, vol. ii.* (1887), *page* 552.
[2] *De Fonblanque's text reads* "*up the country.*" *Words in brackets do not appear in Mr. Porter's copy.*

PERCY LETTERS

bellion, for *they* fired first upon the King's Troops, as they were marching quietly along.'. . .

To His Grace,
The D of N^d

XX

To HENRY REVELEY, *Esq., Peckham, Surrey*

[*Boston, May,* 1775.]

Dear REVELEY:

. . . OUR situation is disagreable enough, for we are confined to the town, the Blockade having now continued for about six weeks. You will have heard that we were attacked on the 19th of last month, on our return to this town, by a very numerous body of Rebels, who, notwithstanding they kept up a constant fire upon us, for upwards of 15 m[ile]s, yet only killed [of?] us about 40 men. They have lately amused themselves with burning the houses upon an island just under the Admiral's nose, & a schooner, with 4 carriage guns & some swivels, which he sent to drive them off, unfortunately got aground, & the Rebels have burnt her. This is not the most agreable thing that could have happened. As our generals have now arrived, I take it for granted that something will be undertaken. I wish

---

[1] *Lord* DARTMOUTH *to the* DUKE OF NORTHUMBERLAND.

LORD Dartmouth presents his comp^{ts} to the Duke of North^d, & has the honor to send His Grace two extracts from private letters from Boston, wh have been communicated to him. . . . "Ld Percy has acquired great honor, he was in every place of danger, cool, deliberate, & wise in all his orders.". . . "Ld Percy commanded & behaved with distinguished honor, & tho he was continually in a shower of bullets, & an object that was much aimed at on horseback, came off unhurt."
Blackheath, 11 *June,* 1775.

we may succeed, as it is necessary to give them a good Blow at first. . . .

          . . . PERCY.

XXI

To the DUKE OF NORTHUMBERLAND

         Boston, June 19, 1775.

My dearest Father:

THO' I am always desirous to write to you by every oppor'y, yet am I more eager to do it after every little action, in order to inform you that I am perfectly safe & well.

On the 17th Gen. Howe, at the head of the Gren^s and Lt Inf'y, & about 2000 men of the Battalions, passed over to Cha^stown, in order to dislodge the Rebels from thence, where they had flung up a very strong intrenchment in order to annoy both this Town & the shipping.

This he effected after a very obstinate engagement, & drove them totally off the Peninsula. As the Rebels had there between 14 & 15000 men intrenched up to the chins, & stood the assault in the redoubt, the affair was a very bloody one on both sides. My Reg^t, being one of the first that entered the redoubt, is almost entirely cut to pieces: there are but 9 men left[1] in my co, & not above 5 in one of the others. None of my officers were killed, tho' a great many wounded, amongst

---

[1] *De Fonblanque's text reads: "there are not nine men left." He explains the words "my company" as a company raised by Lord Percy to bring up his regiment to the war establishment when ordered on active service. The colonel was usually captain of a company which was under the immediate command of a captain-lieutenant. This was true in America also for a time after the war opened.*

wh no. is Mr. Charleton's son. I flatter myself, however, that it will be attended with no bad consequences. For my own part, I had no share in this action, being upon duty in the lines on that day, so that I was only entertained by a pretty smart cannonade, wh we kept up from there upon Roxbury, in order to amuse the Rebels on that side.

If you shd see Lord Huntingdon, I beg you will inform him that his nephew, Lord Rawdon, is perfectly safe & well.

As my Capt of Grenadiers was wounded pretty early in the day, Ld Rawdon commanded my Grenadier Co. during most part of the engagement, & has distinguished himself in a most remarkable manner.

By the best acc'ts I can as yet get of the matter, we had about 100 men killed in this action, & the Rebels above 3 times that n°.

The principal killed on their side is Dr. Warren, Pres't of the Provincial Congress, and on ours poor Maj^r Pitcairn, who commanded the two battalions of marines, & about whom I wrote to my mother.

As money is extremely difficult to be got here, at any rate, I shd think myself particularly obliged to you if you wd order Messrs. H. to send me out by the first safe conveyance coming directly to this port, 500 guineas; but if there is any difficulty in getting that quantity of the coin out, the same sum in Portugal pieces will do, provided they are all of the full weight: as otherwise they will not pass here. . . .

. . . PERCY.

PERCY LETTERS

XXII

To General Harvey (?)

Boston, July 28, 1775.

Genl:

HERE we are still cooped up, and now so surrounded with lines & works as not to be able to advance into the country without hazarding too much. For our army is so small that we cannot even afford a victory, if it is attended with any loss of men. The Rebels have now grown so daring as to make descents on the Islands in the harbor, & carry off the cattle even under the guns of our fleet. About 3 weeks ago they burned the Light House here.

I must own, I cannot help thinking myself particularly fortunate that my rank in the army makes it only my duty to obey, without entitling me to be consulted on any occasion, for I can't say I either approve of our present system or measures, but as they have been formed by more experienced heads than mine, I must not doubt but they are right.

However, every blockhead will form an opinion of his own, & I hope you will excuse me for having mine.

I confess I shd have tho't it a more eligible system, to take advantage of the great Hudson's River to have carried the war into the heart of the country (as a war was inevitable), rather than to have remained here without magazines in a country wh is so penetrated by hills, woods, & ravines, as makes it the most favorable spot in the world for the irregular, undisciplined troops of the rebels. . . . We cd then have kept up communication with Canada, & shut off the supplies from New Engl. This idea is in some measure taken from that of Marshal Saxe, in the conquest of Poland, wh I must own always pleased me, & not the less now that it has been almost wholly followed by the King of Prussia.

XXIII

To the Rev. THOMAS PERCY

Camp on Mount Whoredom, Augt. 12. 1775.

A STRANGE Place Dear D^r. to write from to a Clergyman — Yet so it is, My Tent is upon the highest Summit of it. Know then that there is a ridge of Hills so called running from the Harbour towards the Center of the Town, on which my Brigade is encamped. Was I not certain that you would attribute my silence to the true Cause, want of time, I should fill this Paper with Apologies for my not answering your Letters more regularly. But I will say no more on that Subject, & only thank you in this One for about twenty, which I have received from you. Nothing can make me happier than the News I have from all hands of my Mother's Recovery. I must confess I was very much alarmed at the different Accounts I have lately had of Her bad State of Health. I have wrote to my Brother by this opportunity to congratulate Him on His Wedding. My Father writes me word She is well spoken of.[1]

---

[1] *Lord Algernon Percy married, June* 8, 1775, *Isabella Susannah, second daughter of Peter Burrell of Beckenham, Kent, sister of the first Lord Gwydyr. Writing to Dr. Percy from Newcastle in*

I hope they will be happy. I must own I could have wished for your Sake that there had been a little more of the *Decus et Tutamen Avorum*. However the Pedigree is in good hands when it is in yours.

A curious Event has taken place here yesterday. Our Admiral has been boxing in the Street with one of the Commissioners of the Customs. I have not heard the true History of the Affair, but from what I can gather I believe the Admiral has had the worst of it in every respect. Pray make my *bacio los manos* to Reveley & Madame on the Birth of their Daughter. I hope they got my Letter soon enough.

If you should see M[r]. Charleton, or anybody from North[d]. House should have occasion to write to Him pray let him know that his Son is doing very well & assure Him that a Toe more or less is of no consequence whatever. As for poor Gair he is very ill. So ill that I assure you I am a good [?] alarmed about Him. I should be particularly sorry to lose Him, for He is not only a perfectly well bred Gentleman, but holds a very high Rank in his Profession, & is in great esteem amongst all the Medical Persons here.

Adieu My Dear D[r]. make my best Comp[ts]. acceptable to all your Family & be assured I am

Your sincere Friend
PERCY.

To
  The Rev[d]. & D[r]. PERCY.

1778, Lord Percy said that unless he could find "*a second Lady Algernon*" *he would not be easily tempted to marry again* (*his first marriage having been an unhappy one*). *In* 1779 *Lord Percy married Lady Algernon's younger sister.*

PERCY LETTERS

XXIV

To the DUKE OF NORTHUMBERLAND

Boston, Aug. 18, '75.

[*My dearest*] Father:

... I HAVE enclosed a newspaper containing copies of some letters wrote by some of the principal people at the Congress, wh were intercepted by us. They will lay open to you in a good measure the intention of that Congress on wh Eng. seems to depend for reconciliation. You will perceive from them that their aim is (what I am convinced it has ever been) Independence.

What their European friends will say for them, now, I can't tell.

XXV

To HENRY REVELEY, *Esq.*

Boston, Oct. 29, 1775.

Dear REVELEY:

... NOTHING material has happened here since the 17th June, except the other night an experiment wh the Rebels tried with a piece of cannon or two in a flat-bottomed boat. With these they fired 15 or 20 shot thro' our camp into the Town, when alas, one of the cannon burst, blew up the boat, & sent most of the crew to the Devil.[1]

---

[1] *Samuel Haws, an American private, wrote in his diary October 17th:* "At night our floating Baterys went up towards the canon [Common?] and fired 13 shots but unlucky for them one of their 9 pounders split and killed one man dead and wounded 8 more."

PERCY LETTERS

Our weather is now very rainy and cold: I promise you a tent is no very agreeable habitation just now; & I fear it will be some time before we get into quarters. The Rebels have built Barracks for their Raggamuffins all round us, so that I suppose they intend to be our neighbors for *this* winter. I don't believe they will be very troublesome ones.[1] . . .

Y^r sincere fd
& Aff cousin PERCY.

XXVI

To GENERAL HALDIMAND [2]

Boston, Dec. 14th, 1775.

Dear Sir:

SINCE I did myself the pleasure of writing to you last, our situation is exactly the same. The Rebels, however, have been too fortunate in other places. Canada, as you will have been already informed, is in their hands. Besides this, they have been very successful at sea, having taken a brig loaded with military stores, and — what was to them still a greater

---

[1] *A few words about Percy's relatives, of no general interest, have been omitted at the beginning and end of the letter.*

[2] *General Sir Frederick Haldimand, K. B., was born in Switzerland in 1718, and saw service in Holland before coming to America in 1758. He was in command in Florida from 1766 to 1778, except for a short period in New York, and a journey to England in August, 1775, to give information on the condition of the colonies. As Governor of Canada from 1778 to 1784 he is said to have been harsh and arbitrary. The General died in the canton of Neufchâtel, June 5, 1791.*

Captain Evelyn, who was stationed in Boston in 1774, wrote, October 31st: "Mr. Bourmaster is just come in with his transports from New York, bringing General Haldimand." (Scull's Evelyn, page 34.)

prize—a ship from Glasgow with great quantities of blanketing, woollens, and gloves, all which they were before in great want of. As they have yesterday begun to fling up a work on Phip's Farm, just opposite to Barton's Point, I fancy they mean to bring the mortar which they took in the ordnance brig. If they do, they may trouble us a good deal, as they are within about 1000 yards of the Town. It is very odd that Great Britain still persists in sending out vessels to this part of the world unarmed. The Transports with the troops from Ireland are not yet arrived. One, indeed, with 4 Companies of the 17th Reg., came in here about 6 weeks ago; we imagine the rest are gone to the West Indies. Our Discipline is exactly the same as when you left us, which we shall begin to perceive now the Troops have got into winter quarters. I am extremely happy to find that your reception in London was agreeable to you; you merited it. I had no doubt that His Majesty would do what was proper. I assure you, you are by no means forgot by your friends on this side the Atlantic. Gen. Howe, in the handsomest manner, in the Augmentation, appointed your nephew a 2nd Lieut. in his own Reg., imagining, as you had desired he might do duty with it, that such a step would be agreeable to you; and yesterday he very obligingly appointed him a full Lieutenant in the 45th Reg., chusing particularly that Corps, as there were two situations vacant; by which means your nephew would have a Lieutenant under him, and therefore would not be broke, tho' the youngest Company should be again reduced.

I have had the pleasure of being acquainted with L^{t}. Col. Monkton, and shall take care to particularly recommend Mr. Haldimand to his care. Adieu, my dear Gen. Keep yourself

warm this cold weather, and be assured I am, with greatest truth,
> *Your sincere friend*
> *And humble servant,*
> Percy.

I beg you will be kind enough to make my very best compliments to Capt. Dorkins, and tell him the Engineers have not found it necessary to alter his works in the least, which have been found remarkably useful.[1]

XXVII

To the Rev. Thomas Percy

Boston Jan^{ry} 7th. 1776.

Dear D^R.

YOU will easily see how very irregularly the Letters from Europe arrive, when I inform you, that I did not receive your Letter of the 2^d. of Septr. till yesterday. Having settled this Point, allow me to wish you & your Family the Compliments of the Season, which I hope to do in Person next year, for I take it for granted the next Campaign will be so active & I hope so decisive a One that the Rebels will be glad to sue for Mercy. All however will depend on Our having a Sufficient Force sent Us out very early in the Spring. As Genl. Clinton is just going to set out on a detached Command,

---

[1] *Given in C. W. Tuttle's Capt. Francis Champernowne, The Dutch Conquest of Acadie, and other Historical Papers* (Boston, 1889), *page* 259. *Original in Haldimand Papers, Canadian Archives. See Calendar, page* 525, *no.* 229.

I shall be the only Maj^r. Genl. left under M^r. Howe, so that I shall have business enough. If the Patriots were here, they would abuse Us, & say the Scotch influenced the Cabinet here as well as at home, for Brig^r. Genl. Grant directs Our Commander in Chief & all his Operations. M^r. Howe is I believe the only Man in his Army who does not perceive it. I know the Brig^r. well, & am certain that his Abilities are not equal to what he has undertaken that is the being Director General to the Commander in Chief of such an Army as Ours. I wish from my Soul that we may not feel the Consequences. I have not the least Guess by what Conveyance this Letter is to go, but it shall be by the very first. Our new Admiral is arrived, & like all other new Brooms seems to promise to sweep clean. We wanted a more Active man than the last, for really the Service suffered material during his Command. M^r. Shuldam[1] is a Man well spoken of in his Profession, & therefore I hope we shall go on well. We have had the most violent Gales of Wind for some time past that ever was known, so that we suppose great numbers of the Ships destined for this Port, are gone to the West Indies. Adieu Dear D^r. make my Comp^{ts}. to all your Family & believe me to be

                                          Your's sincerely
                                                 PERCY.

D^r. PERCY
    To
        The Reverend
            D^r. PERCY.

[1] *Admiral Molyneux Shuldham.*

PERCY LETTERS

[*On the night of March 4th Washington fortified Dorchester Heights, which overlooked the town. Howe ordered Percy to storm the American works, but soon changed his plans. Percy wrote March 6th: " It is determined to evacuate this town. I believe Halifax is to be our destination." The British troops left Boston on the 17th of March.*]

XXVIII

To the Rev. THOMAS PERCY

Halifax, June 1*st*. 1776.

Dear D*R*.

ALLOW me to return you many thanks for the Letters I have had the Pleasure of receiving lately from You. I cannot express how much I feel myself obliged to you for all the News you are so good as to give me. The History of the Ladies Head-dress is really entertaining. I did not think my Fair Countrywomen would have made themselves so ridiculous.

I hope the Cabbages Potatoes &c. will be displaced, & that some Heroic Damsel will instead of them grace Her Head with a representation of the Actions at Lexington or Bunkers Hill, or the Flight of the Rebels from before Quebeck.[1] The Niger Man of War brought us yesterday the last agreable Piece of News. And so precipitate was their Retreat that whole Companies flung away even their Arms. Nay they left their Pots boiling, so that the King's Troops set down & eat their dinners for them. As I take for granted you will have the Particulers of this Affair from Canada long before the Arrival

---

[1] *After the failure of the attack upon Quebec, and Montgomery's death, December* 31, 1775, *Arnold spent the winter near the city. In the spring the British commander received reënforcements and was able to drive the Americans out of Canada.*

of this Letter, I shall not trouble you with a Detail of them. I hope I shall soon be able to send you some good News from our Quarter. We are to sail on Wednesday or Thursday next, & I think in about a fortnight after that, something must pop between us & the Rebels.

Adieu Dear D^r. make my best Comp^{ts}. acceptable to M^{rs}. Percy & your Family & believe me to be

Your sincere Friend
PERCY.

P: S: Since writing the above Capt. Mowatt is just arrived & has brought me two Letters more from you, for which I return you many thanks.

To
    The Rev^d. D^r. PERCY.

[*From Halifax the British army sailed for New York, landed at Staten Island late in June, and a month later took Brooklyn, which, with Staten Island, forms the entrance to the inner harbor of New York.*]

XXIX

To the DUKE OF NORTHUMBERLAND

N°. 20th: *New Town Long Island*
Sep^{tr}. 1st. 1776.

ALLOW me my dearest Father to congratulate You on a Victory[1] the King's Troops obtain'd over the Rebels at

[1] *The battle of Brooklyn or Long Island.*

PERCY LETTERS

Bedford near Brookland on the 27th of last Month; which both in its immediate & consequential Effects, is likely to be of the greatest Advantage to Great Britain. On the 26th at Night We marched from Utrecht on this Island, where we had landed without Opposition, & passing thro' Fletlands made for a Gorge in the Mountains which We flattered ourselves was not Guarded, in order to gain the left Flank of the Enemy. This Plan succeeded even beyond our Expectations, for we were on the Flank, & in their Rear, before they knew what we were about. The Engagement did not begin till the advanced Guard under Genl. Clinton & Lord Cornwallis had arrived at Bedford, & before I could get up with the Army the Affair was over. I had however an Opportunity of sending the light Infantry of the Guards to attack a Party of the Rebels, but they ran away directly & only allow'd the Guards just Time to give them one Fire, our loss on this Occasion is scarce to be mentioned. We had only five Officers & fifty seven Men killed, & about 20 Officers wounded. In short our whole Loss in killed, wounded, & missing, does not exceed 300 Men, Whereas on the Rebel side by the very best Acc^{ts}. from themselves they have lost upwards of 3000 Men. We have taken three Gen^{ls}. besides a surprizing Number of Field & other Officers & 1500 Private Men Prisoners. This was intirely owing to our Men attacking them the proper Way. The moment the Rebels fired our Men rushed on them with their Bayonets & never gave them Time to load again — Our Men behaved themselves like British Troops fighting in a good Cause. I cannot Omit mentioning the Guards at whose Head I had the Honor to be — that Day. The Spirit & Alertness of both Officers & Men deserve the highest Encomiums. Their readiness & willingness to do whatever they were desired, has gained them the Esteem & Approbation of the whole Army. In short they are not only the finest Body of Men that ever was seen, but it seems to be the Study of every Officer & Man amongst them to be as distinguishable for Discipline, Spirit, & Conduct, Nothing is a Hardship, nothing is a difficulty with Them. Whatever they are directed to do, they do with Chearfullness & Pleasure. I am happy to be able to do them this Justice which they richly deserve & I am sure his Majesty must be pleased to hear that His Guards have proved themselves worthy of the Honor they enjoy of being near His Person when at Home, by their very proper & spirited Conduct when in the Field. On the 30th. about 3 in the Morn^g. the Rebels evacuated or rather fled from all their strong works at Brookland & passed over to New York, leaving behind them, Cannon, Stores, Horses, Provisions & even most of their Tents. And giving us up by this means quiet Possession of Long Island. In consequence of which We marched on Yesterday to this Place, where almost every body has come in to Us, such as have been in Arms or Active have surrendered Themselves, & all taken the Oaths, Whole Reg^{ts}. we are informed have deserted from them at New York, & in short they are in the greatest State of Confusion. They feel severely the Blow on the 27th. & I think I may venture to assert, that they will never again stand before us in the Field. Every Thing seems to be over with Them, & I flatter myself now that this Campaign will put a total End to the War. I own it will on many Acc^{ts}. give me great Satisfaction if that should be the Case but on none more, than because it will afford me an Opportunity soon of convincing You in Person with what sincerity I am

> *Your most dutifull*
> *& most Affectionate Son*
> Percy.

Maj^r. Cuyler one of Genl. Howe's Aid de Camps will be good enough to present this to you. If you should see L^d. or L^y. Aylesford[1] I beg you will be so good as to tell them, that M^r. Finch is going on remarkably well & is perfectly safe & unhurt.

XXX

To Lord George Germain[2]

[*New Town, Long Island, Sept. 2nd,* 1776.]

AMIDST the various congratulations which your lordship will receive on account of the victory gained over the rebels by His Majesty's troops on the 27th of last month,[3] together with its subsequent effects, permit me to add my tribute. Nor should I have presumed to trouble your lordship even now had not my father acquainted me with the very flattering manner in which you have been pleased to mention my conduct. Praise from your lordship I own I am proud of, and

---

[1] *Lady Aylesford was the sister of Algernon, seventh duke of Somerset, Percy's grandfather. The son, Edward Finch, became colonel of the Twenty-second Regiment.*
[2] *Lord George Germain, son of the first duke of Dorset, was born in 1716. He was appointed by Lord North in 1775 Secretary of State for the Colonies, which position he held until 1782, supporting the ministry's vigorous policy against America.*
[3] *The battle of Brooklyn or Long Island.*

be assured I shall always be happy to lend my aid and assistance in support of Government under an honest and able Minister. The affair of the 27th, my lord, was ably planned and nobly executed. The behaviour of both officers and men on that occasion did honour to the country they came from and to the cause in which they are engaged. The rebels have severely felt the blow, and I think I may venture to foretell that this business is pretty near over. I hope sincerely it is, and that your lordship will soon enjoy the blessings of your country from having delivered it from the most dangerous and unprovoked rebellion that ever existed, by your very proper and spirited measures.[1]

XXXI

To a Gentleman in London

Camp at Newtown, September 4, 1776.

... It was the General's orders that the troops should receive the Rebels' first fire,[2] and then rush on them before they had recovered their arms, with their bayonets, which threw them into the utmost disorder and confusion, they being unacquainted with such a manœuvre. A light dragoon, discovering three riflemen in a wood, who had secreted themselves in order to pick out the officers as they appeared, attacked them, shot one, took the other two prisoners, and brought them to Lord Percy, who rewarded him for his gallant behaviour. A great many of the

---

[1] *Ninth report of the Royal Commission on Historical Manuscripts, part iii., page* 85.
[2] *At the battle of Long Island.*

PERCY LETTERS

horses belonging to Preston's regiment, that were left in Boston at the evacuation, were found on Long-Island.[1] . . .

XXXII

To Lord GEORGE GERMAIN

[*New York, Oct.* 30*th*, 1776.]

ON Genl. Howe's marching to the Continent I was left to defend the island with three British brigades and one Hessian. One of them encamped near New York, and the rest defended our redoubts in the north part of the island.

The day the Genl. left us the rebels came down with about 8,000 men and cannon, as if they meant to attack us; but I knew them too well to imagine any such thing. I let them therefore remain, as they did not chuse to come within canon shot; and when they were tired they returned again to their camp. Nothing happened from that time to the 27th,[2] when in consequence of orders from G^l. Howe I marched with six British and two Hessian reg^{ts} to feel their lines, and at the same time favor a moment [movement?] of Genl Kniphausen's by drawing their attention this way. I approached therefore with caution, for I had not force enough to attack them. By the time I had advanced within random musket shot, their lines (three in number) were all completely manned. These lines are from the middle to the summit of a high mountain, one behind the other with square redoubts at about a 100

---

[1] *Force's American Archives*, 5th series, *vol. ii.*, column 168.
[2] *Percy was left at Harlem Heights while Howe tried to get in Washington's rear. Washington withdrew to White Plains and was defeated there on the 28th.*

yards from each other, the whole supported by Fort Washington, a large square fort with bastions and 18 pounders.[1]

As our moving forward did not make them evacuate their works, I tried what a few shots from six-pounders and shells from two howitzers would do, but they were too well secured by their parapets. About one o'clock in the afternoon they were perceived bringing down canon from their fort into their advanced lines, I left piquets in the former position, and retired with the main body about half way between their works and ours.

My left (being the two Hessian reg^s) occupied a height close to the North River, which commanded a plain to its right, in this plain I placed two reg^s with their right to another hill, where a reg^t and the haubitzers were posted, the remainder of our force extended from thence across Harlaem plains towards the East River, or as there called Harlaem Creek. The rebels now began to canonade us, and as their shot went over the British reg^t the most to the left, I retired a little out of reach. (The other reg^s covered with a stone wall and trees were secure). The two hills were much too strong for them to attack, and as they flanked the plains where the other reg^s were, I thought my position secure. That night I began to work on the two hills, ordered the troops to send for their tents as if I proposed remaining, and talked of the most desperate intentions; it had not however the desired effect, for the rebels who were at least 5,000 in number, posted in such strong lines would not stir. They sent down in the morning (as they had

[1] "*Those ships came up, it seems, to enfilade our lines below that fort, whilst Lord Percy attacked them, which he did three different times, but was as often repulsed by the garrison of Fort Washington.*" (General George Clinton, October 31, 1776. *In Force's American Archives*, 5th series, vol. ii., column 1312.)

done the evening before), a number of their rangers to pop at our advanced posts and sentries, and now and then fired a few canon shot.

Having now fully answered the Gen^{ls}. intentions, and being indeed unable to remain longer on account of the smallness of our numbers and the consequence of the island of New York which this corps was left to guard, I determined to return to the old position in our lines as soon as the evening favored the retreat. This certainly was a very delicate operation, with a small body just under the enemy's nose, some of our advanced piquets within a hundred yards of theirs, and our sentries within 30 or 40.

In the first place I kept my intentions quite to myself, and till 4 o'clock in the afternoon, (at 8 I intended move), I did not open my lips even to Genl. Jones next in command; I only sent him word I would call on him; at a quarter before six I ordered the reg^s under arms, and the commanding officers of the reg^s to come to me; I then gave each the dispositions for the retreat, and their route, ordering the piquets to be left till I sent to take them off, and settled such signals for retiring as could not be mistaken. At six o'clock the retreat was ordered. When the troops were on their march the piquets were taken off silently and in an hour's time the whole returned to their old camp, the enemy not finding we were gone till next morning.

It is very fortunate that in this little excursion of two days not a man suffered by their canon, and only four British soldiers were killed, and three slightly wounded with their musquetry, and three Hessians wounded.

I do assure you I am almost a little vain on this retreat, as the Hessians and all agree in calling the manœuvre a masterly one. The rebels were taken in, for whilst they were observing my manœuvres, Genl. Kniphausen took from them their works at King's bridge which they had left weakly guarded, bringing almost all their forces to oppose me. The attention and obedience to orders in all the troops on that occasion do them the greatest honor, but their silence in getting under arms, and on their return was beyond conception.

Next day the Genl. ordered away the 4th brigade, so only a British and Hessian brigade guard the lines, I am not uneasy as the rebels dare not attack us.[1]

XXXIII

To Henry Reveley, Esq.

New York Island, Nov. 3, 1776.

My dear Reveley:

... News I can send you none. I am detached from the main army with a corps to defend this Island & City, with all our shipping & stores.

Gen. Hare [Howe] has gone to the Continent, & has sent the Rebels to the Devil, or at least the next thing to it, into New Eng^d. Don't tell this to Mr. Wm Vassal, who, I understand, is your neighbor. If ever you see him present my comp^{ts} to him.[2] ...

---

[1] *Ninth report of the Royal Commission on Historical Manuscripts, part iii., page* 86.
[2] *William Vassall graduated at Harvard in* 1733 *and purchased the Cooper estate on Pemberton Hill (now the Square), Boston, in* 1758. *Here he lived in considerable state, and is said to have entertained Lord Percy. He went to England, probably in* 1776, *and was declared banished in* 1778. *He lived at Clapham, within walking distance of Reveley's home at Peckham, and died at Batter-*

PERCY LETTERS

I gave my Friends, the Rebels, a little [start?], this day's sennight. I marched out with part of the army under my command towards their lines, within musket-shot, in order to reconnoitre their forces, & draw their attention towards us, to favor a manœuvre of Lt.-Gen. Kniphausen, who was to endeavor to get into their rear. This had the desired effect, for, whilst they were sending off for re-inforcements to oppose me, who, God knows, did not intend to meddle with them (for they were more than three times my numbers) & besides intrenched up to the eyes in their rows of lines, supported by a very strong Redoubt, Kniphausen just got into the position he wanted.

On Monday eve'g, therefore, having executed my orders, I returned again to my old Camp, without their daring to molest me. In this whole excursion I had but 4 British soldiers killed & 3 wounded. Their cannon were so ill pointed, that tho' they fired annoyingly at us, they hit nobody.[1] . . .

PERCY.

sea Rise, May 8, 1800. The brilliant Lady Holland was a relative of his. Vassall's Boston house became in 1803 the home of Gardiner Greene, brother-in-law of Lord Lyndhurst.

[1] Nothing of public interest has been omitted from this letter.

The ninth report of the Royal Commission on Historical Manuscripts mentions a communication to Lord George Germain, dated at New York, November 29, 1776, enclosing a plan (not now with letter) of "the rebel lines flung up to protect the north part of the island, which were forced by four weak British and two Hessian battalions under Lord Percy's command on the 16th of November." On this day Fort Washington fell, and a winter of disasters for the American cause began.

The Myers collection at the New York Public Library has a letter addressed to Richard Molesworth, Deputy Paymaster-General to the forces under Lord Percy, dated at Newport, April 28, 1777, authorizing the payment of money for the six Hessian regiments under the command of Brigadier-General Lossberg; it is signed by Percy.

NOTE IN CONCLUSION

NOTE IN CONCLUSION

IT is to be regretted that we have no letters describing Percy's brave assault upon Fort Washington and his operations in Rhode Island—events of the period between November 3, 1776, and his departure for England. A ship which sailed from New York on the 23d of March, 1777, for Liverpool carried news that Lord Percy's disagreement with Sir William Howe in matters military was already the subject of gossip, and that Percy wished to be relieved of his command. His great popularity and influence made it possible for the opposition to Government to use this event to embarrass the ministers whose conduct of affairs in America was always open to criticism. Percy, it seems, remained in Rhode Island with a separate command, after the successful expedition against Newport, in which he was associated with Sir Henry Clinton. In this position he expected a force under him sufficient to permit extensive operations which might add to his reputation as a soldier. The campaign in New Jersey at the close of 1776, including Washington's brilliant manœuvres at Trenton and Princeton, made it necessary to draw upon Percy's already inadequate forces. Howe thought that his subordinate did not meet his requisitions promptly and to the letter. Percy's friends, on the other hand, declared that he "behaved like an angel," and that "exalted merit had

NOTE IN CONCLUSION

been exposed to jealousy and envy." The citizens and the rank and file of the army held the latter view.

Having obtained a recall, Percy went on board the Mercury packet at Rhode Island early in May, 1777, and reached Falmouth, England, on the 2d of June, after a passage of twenty-eight days.[1] Upon his arrival in London he waited upon Lord George Germain, "who immediately ordered his postchaise and took him to Kew, where he was most graciously received, and had an audience with His Majesty near two hours."[2] Lord Percy's arrival aroused criticism of the ministry among those who believed that his withdrawal from America was due to his disapproval of the management of the war or to jealousy on the part of Sir William Howe, and that Percy could have been persuaded to continue in service against the Colonies. In less than three months he was made a Lieutenant-General in the army.

In the autumn Lord Percy, now a peer in his own right through the death of his mother, moved the address to the King in the House of Lords, speaking in a voice scarcely audible. He had a word of praise for Howe, and for officers who served in America under difficulties, far from those who so readily criticised their actions. He expressed great sorrow for the occasion of the war, but felt that it must go on until the Colonies bowed before the rights of Great Britain and the

---
[1] "*The Howes are not in fashion. Lord Percy is come home disgusted by the younger.*" (Horace Walpole to Sir Horace Mann, *June* 18, 1777.)
[2] *London Chronicle, June* 5–7 *and* 7–10, 1777.

NOTE IN CONCLUSION

superior power which upheld them. At other times he was very discreet and reserved in his comments on the war.[1]

As Duke of Northumberland he continued to show an interest in military affairs, although in later years an affliction of the gout forced him to withdraw from active life.

[1] *Horace Walpole to Sir Horace Mann, July* 17, 1777.

INDEX

INDEX

A

ADAMS, John, delegate to Congress, 36.
Adams, Samuel, delegate to Congress, 36.
Andrews, John, quoted, 34.
Andrews, Mrs. Ruthy, her sketches of Boston, 28.
Army, British, in Massachusetts in August, 1774, 31, 36; at battle of Long Island, 69.
Aylesford, Charlotte, Countess of, 70.

B

Barnard, Lieutenant-Colonel Berry, wounded, 53.
Bernard, Sir Francis, his house, 34.
Boston, people of, 27, 31; views of, 28; army at, in 1774, 31, 34, 36; Percy's house, 34; lighthouse burned, 58; Mount Whoredom, 59; siege of, 62; evacuation, 66.
Boston Port Bill, 29.
Bunker Hill, battle of, 56, 57.
Burrell, Peter, father of Lady Algernon Percy, 59; father of second Countess Percy, 60.

C

Cambridge, affairs at, in 1774, 41.
Canada, taken by Americans, 62.
Castle William, soldiers at, 36.
Charlestown, 41, 42.
Charleton, Mr., his son wounded, 57, 60.
Clergy, attitude of, 29.
Climate of Boston, 29, 49.
Clinton, Sir Henry, to have a detached command, 64; at Long Island, 68.
Clinton, Lord Thomas Pelham, a candidate for Parliament, 17.
Coin, scarcity of, 57.
Colonies (American), people of, 28, 44; condition of, in November, 1774, 43, 44.
Cooper, Grey, on the Boston Port Bill, 29; note on, 46.
Crops in Massachusetts, 33.
Cushing, Thomas, delegate to Congress, 36.
Cuyler, Major Cornelius, 70.

D

Danvers, soldiers at, 36.
Dartmouth, Lord, sends news of Percy to his father, 55.
Desertion, decreasing, 36.
Drummond, Lord, on Percy's part in the retreat from Lexington, 53, 54.

E

Evelyn, William Glanville, quoted, 34, 62.
Exeter, New Hampshire, 46.

INDEX

F

Fanthrop, William, trial of, 39.
Fifth Regiment of Foot, reaches Boston, 27; trouble in, 39.
Finch, Edward, mentioned, 70.
Fort Hill, Boston, soldiers at, 36.
Fort Washington, 73; fall of, 76.
Fort William and Mary, taken, 47.
Francia, Lieutenant, 27.

G

Gage, General Thomas, Percy's opinion of, 25; at Saiem, 28; has done his duty, 28; his lenity, 37; in need of troops, 42; to Lord Dartmouth on Percy's part in the retreat from Lexington, 53.
Gair, Doctor, his illness, 60.
Germain, Lord George, his career, 70; receives Percy, 80.
Grant, Brigadier-General James, his influence over Howe, 65.

H

Haldimand, Sir Frederick, at Boston, 42; his career, 62; his nephew promoted, 63.
Harvey, General Edward, note on, 47.
Haws, Samuel, quoted, 61.
Head-dress of women, 1776, 66.
Horses, American, 33.
Howe, Sir William, promotes Haldimand's nephew, 63; under Grant's influence, 65; and Percy disagree, 79.
Hudson River, strategic value of, 58.

I

Independence, the aim of Congress, 61.

J

Jones, Colonel, arrives from Quebec, 43.

K

King, Ensign Henry, 27.
Knyphausen, General Baron Wilhelm von, takes King's Bridge, 75, 76.

L

Lexington, retreat from, official account, 49; unofficial account, 52.
Long Island, battle of, 67–72.
Lossberg, Baron Friedrich Wilhelm von, 76.

M

Magistrates, protection of, 36; not allowed to act, 38.
Massachusetts, climate, 29; the country, 32; crops, 33; the Council, 35; under the Regulation Acts, 35; delegates to Congress, 36; in rebellion, 37, 38; raising an army, 41.
Massachusetts, people of. *See* Colonies, people of.
Molesworth, Richard, 76.
Monkton, Lieutenant-Colonel Robert, 63.

[86]

INDEX

Mount Whoredom, a hill in Boston, 59.
Mowatt, Captain Henry, 67.

N

Newcastle, New Hampshire, fort near, taken, 46.
New England, people of. *See* Colonies, people of.
New York, manœuvres about, 72.
Non-importation talked of, 37.
Northumberland, Elizabeth, Duchess of, furthers election of her son Earl Percy, 19; collects views, 28; her health, 59.
Northumberland, Sir Hugh (Smithson) Percy, Duke of, 15, 30; obtains permission for Percy to return to England, 47.

O

Oxen, American, 33.

P

Paine, Robert Treat, delegate to Congress, 36.
Palmer, Robert, died coming out to Boston, 27.
Parliamentary election for Westminster, 16–20.
Percy, Lord Algernon, his marriage, 59.
Percy, Lady Algernon, 59, 60.
Percy family, and the Reveley family, 30.

Percy, Hugh, Earl, his letters, where found, 7, 8; his ancestry, 15; political opinions, 16; a candidate for Parliament, 16–20; his letter quoted, 18; later life, marriages, character, 21; opinion of Gage, 25; reaches Boston, 26, 27; his house, 34; entertains, 34; attitude toward Administration, 34; and the Fanthrop trial, 39; sends for books, 44; reported dead, 45; declines to return to England, 47; in the retreat from Lexington, 49–55; writes of Bunker Hill battle, 56; criticises the campaign, 58; his second marriage, 60; in Halifax, 66; and the battle of Long Island, 68, 71; about New York, 72; before Fort Washington, 73; order for money, 76; disagreement with Howe, 79; arrival in England, 80; remarks on the war, 80.
Percy's Regiment. *See* Fifth Regiment of Foot.
Percy, Rev. Thomas, ancestry and career, 25.
Pigott, Colonel Robert, 28, 31.
Pitcairn, Major John, killed at Bunker Hill battle, 57.
Pomeroy, Colonel Seth, 41.
Porter, Rev. Edward Griffin, his visit to Alnwick, 8; death prevented use of Percy's letters, 9.
Portsmouth, New Hampshire, affairs at, 46.
Preble, Colonel Jedediah, 41.

INDEX

Q

Quebec, attack upon, 66.

R

Rawdon, Lord, 27; at Bunker Hill battle, 57.
Regulation Acts, 35, 37, 42.
Reveley family, 30.
Reveley, Henry, birth of a daughter, 60.
Revere, Paul, warns Portsmouth, 46, 47.
Revolutionary War, Percy on the, 71.
Roxbury, 41, 42.

S

Salem, soldiers at, 36.
Saxe, Marshal, referred to by Percy, 59.
Seymour, Lady Elizabeth, her marriage, 15, 30. *See also* Northumberland, Duchess of.
Ships, captured, 62, 63.
Shuldham, Admiral Molyneux, his character, 65.
Smith, Lieutenant-Colonel Francis, wounded, 53.
Smithson, Sir Hugh. *See* Northumberland, Duke of.
Solemn League and Covenant, 29.
Sons of Liberty, 45.

T

Trees in Massachusetts, 32.
Tuttle, Charles Wesley, his book referred to, 64.

V

Vassall, William, note on, 75.

W

Walpole, Horace, quoted, 19, 49, 80, 81.
Ward, Colonel Artemas, 41.
Warren, Joseph, killed at Bunker Hill battle, 57.
White Plains, battle at, 72.
Worcester, militia at, in 1774, 37.